John Henry
NEWMAN

Heart to Heart

John Henry
NEWMAN
Heart to Heart

Rev. Vincent Giese

*Christmas blessings,
1993, Rev. Vince Giese*

New City Press

To
J. Edgar Thibodeau,
a Catholic layman, a Newman scholar,
and a warm-hearted friend, whose donation
of over 200 volumes by and about Newman
provided the sources of this book.

New City Press, 86 Mayflower Ave., New Rochelle, NY 10801
©1993 New City Press
Printed in the United States of America

Cover picture: a portrait by an unknown author of John Henry
Newman (1879), San Giorgio in Velabro, Newman's diaconal
church in Rome.

Library of Congress Cataloging-in-Publication Data:

Giese, Vincent J.
    John Henry Newman : heart to heart / Vincent Giese.

    Includes bibliographical references.
    ISBN 1-56548-023-6 : $6.95
    1. Newman, John Henry, 1801-1890. 2. Catholic Church—
England—Clergy—Biography. 3. Authors, English—19th century—
Biography. I. Title.
    282'.092—dc20
[B]   92-42030

Contents

Introduction

When the Vatican Congregation of Saints decreed on the heroic sanctity of John Cardinal Henry Newman on January 21, 1991, in Rome, Pope John Paul II declared John Henry Newman Venerable.

Thus the most celebrated of Anglican converts to Roman Catholicism, whose life spanned nearly the entire nineteenth century, was recognized by the Holy Father as a man who, to a heroic degree, had practiced the theological virtues of faith, hope and charity toward God and his neighbor, as well as the cardinal virtues of prudence, justice, temperance and fortitude.

Born in London in 1801, John Henry Newman was received into the Catholic Church on October 9, 1845, by Blessed Dominic Barberi, and was elevated to the cardinalate in 1879 at age seventy-eight by Pope Leo XIII. Newman lived nearly ninety years until he died on August 11, 1890.

John Henry Newman is an intellectual giant of the modern age, so much so that many would like to see him named a Doctor of the Church. His Anglican years covered the time from 1822 until 1845. In 1816 he entered Trinity College at Oxford University, then after graduation became a Fellow at Oriel College. He received Anglican orders of deacon in 1824, priesthood in 1825.

In 1828 Newman was named vicar of St. Mary's

Church, Oxford, where he distinguished himself as preacher and became a leader of the Oxford Movement, a reform movement within the Church of England, which began in 1833 and led him into the Catholic Church in 1845.

During his Catholic years, which spanned another forty-five years, he was ordained a Catholic priest, founded the Oratory of St. Philip Neri in Birmingham and London, established a Catholic University in Dublin in 1850, and in 1864, when he and all Roman clergy were attacked, published a reply, *Apologia Pro Vita Sua*, a defense of his life.

Out of respect for his achievements both as an Anglican and later as a Roman Catholic (his works include some eighty-five books of writings, correspondence and homilies), Newman nevertheless was recognized primarily as a man of prayer because of a complete trust in the providence of God.

During his period of inquiring into the Catholic Church, and guided by his study of the Fathers of the early Church, Newman suffered many anxieties, but he persisted. His study of the development of doctrine led him to conclude the Catholic Church and the Church of the ancient Fathers were one and the same.

Why is there such a worldwide interest in Newman today? Certainly his influence on the Second Vatican Council, seventy-five years after his death, was enormous. He was the most frequently quoted theologian during the Council deliberations, and indeed he has been called the "Absent Father" of the Council. Pope Paul VI attested to the power of Newman's influence on the Second Vatican Council when in the ceremony of the beatification of Blessed Dominic Barberi on October 27, 1963, he linked Blessed Dominic and John Henry Newman as "the two saintly figures." There is no doubt that Pope Paul VI wanted to proclaim Newman a saint, but the long, laborious work on his life and writings had not been completed.

The canonization process was begun in 1958 by Oratorian Father C. S. Dessain, and continued to 1978 when a new historical commission was appointed by the archdiocese of Birmingham and the work began anew under the Rev. Vincent F. Blehl, S.J., postulator, on leave from Fordham University, New York, and the enthusiasm of Father Gregory Winterton, then Provost of the Birmingham Oratory.

All the writings by and about Newman, both as Anglican and a Catholic, had to be gathered and digested in a *positio*, which first had to be approved by the archdiocese of Birmingham, where the case of sainthood originated, then submitted to the Vatican Congregation on the Saints for final approval. This happened in January 21, 1990, a hundred years after Newman's death.

What does Newman offer to the contemporary world? The purpose of this small study suggests that John Henry Newman was indeed the first theologian to define the role of the laity in the Church. I have tried to trace his concern for lay persons in the Church through his work in the Oxford Movement, which brought him to the early conclusion that the alliance between the establishment (state) and the Church of England was corrupting the Church of England. The state in effect was dictating what the Church should be, even to the point of suppressing dioceses in England and Ireland.

When Newman called for a dis-entanglement of the Church of England and the establishment, in the beginning of the Oxford Movement, he was already formulating his view on the role of the laity in the Church which would be proclaimed in the 1960s by the Catholic Church in the Second Vatican Council.

Newman hoped to persuade the clergy, especially the bishops, to get out of politics, particularly out of their linkage with the aristocracy. That was what the Oxford Movement was about—to break the alliance between Church and state.

Apart from the fact that the alliance corrupted the clergy, particularly the bishops, Newman wanted a return to the pastoral concern of the clergy and bishops in caring for souls. It was in a sense to open the middle and the under classes to the spirit of the gospel. The aristocracy, and their bishops, no longer had an exclusive claim to it.

The French Revolution in the eighteenth century had attacked the economic privileges of the higher clergy. To the general surprise, as Christopher Hollis writes, "it was discovered that religion was much more vigorously alive among the underprivileged, lay and clerical, than had been generally understood." Judging from the decline of the main denominations in the West and the growth of the Church in Third World countries, that still seems to be case.

In England after 1815, religion was regarded primarily as the defender of order and the right of property and the unqualified opponent of all reform. The same idea prevailed after 1815 when in reaction to the French Revolution, the papacy frankly was on the side of absolute monarchy as enemies of all revolution and indeed of all reform. In England, it was the Church of England, not the Catholic Church of France, but it was a mood of the times that Newman could not help but be aware of.

In the early days of the Oxford Movement, Newman challenged the conservative system of a national church dependent on the state, in his essays on the primitive Church and the great bishops of antiquity. In his first essay on the primitive Church, Newman wrote: "Hitherto we have been dependent on the state, i.e., on the ruling powers in the country—the king and the aristocracy. But these recollections of the past must not engross our minds, or hinder us from looking at things as they are, and they will be soon, and inquiring what is intended by providence to take the time-honored instrument which he has broken (if it is yet to be broken), the regal and aristocratical power. I shall disgust many men when I say we must look to the people."[1] Newman wanted to show how the popular support of the middle and lower classes might be won again for the Church. It was a call to reform within the Anglican community, just as the Second Vatican Council later on was a call for reform within the Catholic community.

Newman's long study of the Arian heresy strengthened his view that the lay people had a role in preserving truth, at a time when even the Arian bishops had gone astray. Later on, in his Catholic years, when he established the Catholic University in Dublin, his views of the university to train the laity in the relation between philosophy and knowledge was revolutionary. He saw the university as a great center of knowledge, whereas the prevalent Catholic view saw only the seminary and convent as theological centers, from which lay persons were excluded.

Newman insisted upon an educated laity, whose task would be to witness to the modern world in all its aspects. It was Newman's conviction that the clergy should be interested first of all in the spiritual welfare of souls, and not in the political issues of the day, especially in the intrigues between the state and religion. The laity, as he addressed the middle and the under classes, were essential to the whole Church, not just to churchmen whose ideal, in his day, was a good living and a hundred pounds a year.

Again, and most notably, in his brief association with *The Rambler*, a Catholic journal edited by laypersons, his essay "On Consulting the Faithful in Matters of Doctrine," was revolutionary and caused an uproar in both England and Rome. It appeared in 1859 when Newman briefly took over as editor of *The Rambler* at the request of the bishops. More than one hundred years ago, Newman was urging the hierarchy of the Church to look for a *concensus fidelium* (a getting the pulse of a situation) from the laity in doctrinal matters. Already Newman was distinguishing between the power to define the faith (the hierarchy) and the unanimous faith of the baptized (the community).

Newman was urging the Church to consult a body of the faithful before defining a particular dogma.

In fact, as Newman cites, Pius IX gathered opinions of the laity before proclaiming the dogma of the Immaculate Conception, as did Pius XII before defining the Assumption. While the definition of the faith is confided to the successors of the apostles in union with the popes, the development of revelation has been confided to all those who have been baptized in Jesus Christ. It is the holy community of the whole Church that continually develops in knowledge and love.

It is interesting to note that Newman, a product of Victorian England, never particularly concerned himself with the social problems, for example, as did Pope Leo XIII, who raised Newman to the cardinalate. Newman, however, was alone among Catholic leaders to oppose the Crimean War as unjust.

But far more important, he was alone in defending the role of the laity both in the Church and in the modern world. The Catholic Church in England (contrary to Ireland) was very small and had no political power. Even if it had wanted to, it was unlikely to make much of a change in the social problems. To speak out was anathema to Newman's concept of the clergy. But his doctrines on the role of the laity were far reaching, even though ahead of his time. The clergy must minister to the poor, as indeed Newman's life demonstrated in the poor parish of Birmingham. But a well-educated laity must deal with the social issues.

Christopher Hollis, in *Newman and the Modern World*, writes: "Pope John's call for *aggiornamento* did not in any way put him into opposition to his immediate predecessors but it means that his whole conception of the Church was a conception radically different from either Pius IX or Pius X, even though Leo XIII and Benedict XV would not have been unsympathetic. Whereas the earlier Piuses thought the Church as an institution on the defensive and of Catholics as people whose faith was to be protected against a wicked and godless world, Pope John thought of Christ as a bringer of universal love, as a God who had died for all men and whose divine message must be carried to all men."[2] In other words, Pope John XXIII was more sympathetic to Newman than were Pius IX or Pius X. Newman saw into the future.

Pope Paul VI, at the celebration of the beatification of Dominic Barberi, gave this special tribute to Newman. He spoke of Newman as "the promoter and representative of the Oxford Movement . . . who, in full consciousness of his mission, and guided solely by the love of truth and a fidelity to Christ, traced an itinerary, the most toilsome but also the greatest, the most meaningful, the most conclusive that human thought ever travelled during the past century . . . to arrive at the fullness of wisdom and peace."[3]

Hollis concludes. "We can say with Cardinal Gracias that his [Newman's] *Essay on Development*, at its first issue somewhat suspect, has now been almost officially adopted as the doctrine of the Church. We say nearly the same of the *Grammar of Assent*. He pleaded and got himself condemned for the championship of the apostolate of the laity which now is officially proclaimed. Catholic policy is increasingly stamped by his ideas on education. He championed what are today the accepted rights of the scholar in biblical interpretation. He found, in short, the Church at one of the lowest moments of its history a servile society and turned it into a free society."[4]

In the twenty-five or more years since the conclusion of the Second Vatican Council, we have seen the growth of lay participation in the Church. Lectors, ministers of the eucharist, musicians, pastoral councils, parish school

14

boards, on and on. Newman might have shuddered at this turn of events if he were living today, because it is not what he exactly had in mind, when he considered the role of the layperson in the Church. It is really a further development of clericalism in the Church, since most of these ministries are centered in the Church, many of them in the sanctuary, but still have little to do with the community of the world. Politics, business, professions, the marketplace, the community, the family, the neighborhood, is the ambiance of the authentic vocation of the layperson in the world. But Newman insisted on a well-educated, articulate laity for this role.

Today, it seems, the role of the priest, not the prophet as witnesses of the gospel, is still emphasized in our preoccupation with mini-clerics. It is interesting to ask, if Newman were alive today, would he be identified with the institutional Church, or would he be identified with a reform movement, like an Oxford Movement, to reform the Church itself?

We still don't take the laity too seriously, or we would be more open to getting a "sense of the faithful" from laypersons on all issues, be more open to the role of women in the Church, or be listening to the voices of the poor (the Evangelicals are out in front of the mainline Churches), for example, among the Hispanic people in Central America, Mexico, and South America, and even among the Hispanics in our own country.

But once again, at least in the Western nations, we are slowly becoming the Church of the wealthy, not the Church of the poor or even the middle-class (as they come upon hard times). We are now closing lower middle-class and lower-class parochial schools. Even the middle-class is becoming more and more alienated. The recent statement by one American bishop that he would like to close down the chancery office, so he could get out among the people again, rings true in many a bishop's heart. Newman would have loved that remark. The faith of the people has not faltered, but they are more and more disaffected with the institutional Church. We need to listen to the faithful.

Newman also might have problems with the growth of Catholic universities and colleges, and at state universities, Catholic centers named after Newman himself, because he would see Catholic philosophy and theology slowly eroding, considered often as another opinion. It seems as if there is no such thing as a Catholic philosophy or even theology. One seminary, in cutting costs, eliminated courses on Aquinas and Newman.

We have substituted liturgy for doctrine. We are very capable as babysitters for Catholic college students, not as one who gives them an excitement about Catholic religion, or who is committed to entering a dialogue with the departments of the university on the relationship of knowledge to theology, the queen of sciences.

Or, in our local parishes, for example, where we often have a sophisticated RCIA program for those entering the Church, would Newman look upon it as conversion to a sacramental liturgy rather than first of all as a faith conversion, perhaps more beneficial to the Catholic worshiping community than to the convert? Somewhere, again, doctrine has slowly disappeared, as in our schools, our seminaries, and colleges, in our CCD programs, in our instructions to converts, and even in our ecumenical efforts. We are putting too much stress upon personal relationships and not enough on the content of our faith. Again, we need Newman's sense of balance.

Newman, as a first of the ecumenists, felt that the Catholic should be worthy of Christ, and this was primarily a work of God, not of the human person. He was concerned not with whether the convert was worthy of the Church, but whether the Church was worthy of the convert.

A true conversion must be necessarily a slow business, a gradual turning of the whole personality. Organization is important but the obsession with it is dangerous. "We want seminaries far more than Sees," he wrote. "We want education, view, combination, organization—above all view. It is cruel that so many able persons are doing so little."[5] The path of truth was a difficult path. Form after form was tried by him—the Christianity of Evangelicals, the Christianity of Whately, of Hawkins, of Keble and Pusey, but it was not the Christianity of the New Testament and of the first ages.

In the end, it was his personality which was Newman's uniquely ecumenical gift. As Dean Church, a great admirer of Newman, wrote, "Surely never did man break so utterly with the Church, who left so many sympathies behind him, or took so many with him, who continued to feel so kindly and with such large-hearted justice to those from whom his changed position separated him in this world for ever."[6]

If Newman gives us any insight into the ecumenical movement today, as enunciated by the Second Vatican Council, it is common sense. While it is good in itself, as we discover more and more points of identity among the various denominations and stress these and not points of disagreement, Newman reminds us not to be more Roman Catholic than the pope, not more Roman than the Romans. For him, conversion was a process, not a sudden decision, not a sudden outburst of Christ in our hearts—a journey of faith, toward truth. Once he was received by the Catholic Church, Newman wrote that he didn't feel all that different than before. "It was like coming into port after a rough sea."

If I could give a name by which we could honor Venerable John Henry Newman, I would simply call him The Apostle of the Laity in the Church. He might like us to read him in that light.

Chapter One

Newman's Anglican Years at Oxford

The well-known hymn, "Lead Kindly Light," was composed by John Henry Newman in 1833, at the end of a long, lonely illness in Sicily, far from his home in London. The feverish illness, which afflicted Newman, then thirty-two years old, came at the end of a Mediterranean voyage he had made with two friends, Archdeacon Froude and his son Hurrell, at that time Newman's closest friend and fellow-tutor at Oriel College, Oxford University. Originally, Newman had planned to return with the Froudes, but decided to return to Sicily alone for a time.

Newman bought provisions for his journey, hired mules and a servant named Gennaro. Later, in April, he took sick with a fever and stayed at an inn at Leanforth. His faithful servant looked after him and gently nursed him back to health. By late May he was well enough to plan his return home. He departed June 13 for Marseilles, France.

Newman's period of illness was a time of introspection. Weary of his struggle through the wilderness, and homesick, he was at peace, because God was leading him.

Lead, Kindly Light, amidst the encircling gloom,
Lead Thou Me On;
the night is dark and I am far from home,
Lead Thou Me On.
Keep Thou my feet,
I do not ask to see the distant scene:
one step enough for me.

I was not ever thus,
or prayed that Thou shouldst lead me on.
I loved to choose and see my path;
But now lead thou me on, lead thou me on.
I loved the garish day, and 'spite of fears,
pride ruled my will;
remember not past years.

So long Thy power hath blessed me,
sure it still, will lead me on;
O'er moor and fen, o'er crag and torrent til
the night is gone.
And with the morn those Angels smile
Which I have loved long since, and lost awhile.

The fever, as Newman recalled, burned up his past and released new energy when he returned home. He recalls he returned from abroad "with an exuberant and joyous energy, which he had never before experienced—or since."[1]

"And my health and strength came back to me with such a rebound that some friends at Oxford, on seeing me, did not well know it was I, and hesitated before they spoke to me."[2] In his account of the ordeal, he writes, "Well, in an unlooked far away, I came to Sicily and the devil thinks his time has come. I was given over into his hands . . . I could almost think the devil saw I am to be a means of usefulness and tried to destroy me. Now it certainly is remarkable that a new and long sphere of action has opened upon me from the very moment I returned."[3]

Newman reached Oxford, and his mother's house in London, July 9, 1833.

It was the third such spiritual crisis Newman had associated with a feverish illness. His first calling, or vocation sign, came when he was fifteen years old, and it made him a Christian. John Henry Newman was ill from worry about his parents, whose business had failed in 1816. Mr. Newman was a banker. There was turmoil in the family.

Left at school during the holidays, Newman underwent a kind a religious metamorphosis and experienced a moment of conversion, not a violent change, but a state of acknowledging and loving God.

He rested "in the thought of two, and two only, supreme and luminously self-evident beings, myself and my creator,"[4] he wrote later. At that time he also felt called to lead a celibate life. He felt called to a total dedication to God's service, of becoming "a eunuch" for the kingdom of heaven.

A second spiritual crisis came at age twenty-six, when he began to prefer intellectual excellence to moral.

"Lead Thou Me On." For Newman conversion was not a dramatic moment, but a series of steps, of callings. It is a lifetime process. Two months before he penned, "Lead Kindly Light," while on the same Mediterranean voyage, Newman wrote a lesser known poem when he was a pilgrim at the site of St. Paul's martyrdom, at Tre Fontana, Rome.

> Did we but see,
> When life first open'd,
> how our journey lay,
> Between its earliest and it's closing day.
> Or view ourselves, as we one time shall be,
> Who strive for the high prize,
> such sight would break the youthful spirit,
> though bold for Jesus' sake.

> But thou dear Lord, whilst I traced out bright scenes
> that were to come,
> Isaac's pure blessing and a verdant home,
> Didst spare me, and withheld the fearful word;
> walling me year by year,
> till I am found a pilgrim pale,
> With Paul's sad girdle bound.

In his oft quoted sermon on "Divine Calls," Newman said, "For in truth we are not called once only, but many times; all through our life Christ is calling us. He called us first in baptism; but afterward also; whether we obey his voice or not, he graciously calls us still." This turned out to be the story of his own life.

Early Preparation

John Henry Newman was born in the city of London and baptized a few yards away from the Bank of England, early in 1801. He had an hereditary taste for music and

22

an interest in practical and scientific knowledge and mathematics, with a general sense of culture.

His father became a banker and married Jemima Fourdrineer, of a well-known London family known for engraving and paper manufacturing. Throughout his youth, theology was nothing more than the saving of his soul, for his parents intended him for the law.

At a very early age he was sent to Dr. Nicholas, at Ealing, said then to be the best preparatory school in the country. There were three hundred boys there, and many became distinguished. Newman rose to the head of the school.

At the age of twelve he composed an operata. From Dr. Nicholas' he went straight to Trinity College, Oxford. While at Trinity, his father lost his banking job. In the declining fortunes of his family, he heard the call to a higher profession of theology, celibacy and ministry. Not yet nineteen, while he passed his examination for his degree, perhaps due to illness, or to his family problems, when the class list came out, he was under the line, but for three years he remained at Oxford, as a scholar of Trinity College. But his mind and heart were set on Oriel College.

It was in 1822 that Newman was elected to a fellowship at Oriel, a college at Oxford University. His public career had now begun. Newman was then twenty-one years old. He felt that April 12, 1922 to be the turning point of his life. It raised him from obscurity to the need for competency and reputation.

In 1824, Newman took Anglican orders of deacon and became the curate of St. Clement's, a quaint little church at the London approach to Oxford. His church was soon filled and he began to consider a new church on a different site, but he never achieved this. In 1825, he was ordained an Anglican priest.

In 1826 he became a tutor at Oriel College. In 1828 Newman found himself in a college that at that time was in the very front of academic progress, along with his closest friends and fellow tutors, Robert Wilberforce and Hurrel (Richard) Froude, entirely devoted to him. As one friend, Thomas Mozeley, observed, at this point in his life, "it never was possible to be even a quarter of an hour in his company without a man feeling himself to be invited to take an onward step sufficient to tax his energy and faith."

During these early years at Oriel College he developed friendships with John William Bowden, who died in 1844; with Richard Whately, an older man whom Newman felt a deep affection, until they parted because of religious differences, and with Thomas Mozeley. Through Froude, Newman also became intimate with Keble.

In 1926 he was appointed vicar of St. Mary's Church. His parochial sermons and his increasing absorption in the Fathers of the Church during this time occupied Newman the following years. And in 1831 he agreed to write a serious history on *The Arians of the Fourth Century*.

The subject was to influence Newman's thoughts the following years. He saw an analogy between the Arians and the position of the Anglican Church. Convinced of the necessity to belong to the Catholic Church of Tradition, he set out to prove that the Church of England had not lost its Catholic character at the Reformation.

In the fourth century, when many Sees were held by

the Arian bishops, part at least of their flocks remained Catholic.

By June 1832, he had finished the book. He was exhausted, and so it happened when Hurrel Froude was obliged to take a long holiday for health reasons, at the end of the year Newman and the Froudes left for a long Mediterranean tour. He was to be deeply impressed by his first contact with the life of the Catholic Church in Italy, especially in Rome.

The Oxford Movement

Newman's return to Oxford University, after his soul-searching odyssey in the Mediterranean, with renewed energy and vigor, at age thirty-two, was the beginning of a long and fruitful life, until his death at age eighty-nine, in 1890.

One week after his return to Oxford from his Mediter-ranean voyage, precisely, July 14, 1833, the Oxford Movement had its beginning at Oxford University. It was to become for the Church of England what the Second Vatican Council would become for the Catholic Church 129 years later. It became a revitalizing reform move-ment within the Church of England, and which still infuses the Anglican Community.

The Oxford Movement, in Newman's eyes, began when John Keble, a distinguished Fellow at Oriel Col-lege, and friend of Newman, preached the now famous Assize Sermon at St. Mary's Church before the judge of Assize, on the subject of "National Apostasy." Keble defended the Church of England against the proposed suppression by the government of bishoprics, or dioceses, in England and Ireland. Keble called for the Church to be free from state intervention.

The Oxford Movement was a declaration against the alliance of Church and state. He pleaded for all churchmen to separate themselves from the state. There was too much of an alliance between ministers, libertines, the parliament and the bishops. Keble thus gave the first expression to the apostolic idea of "no concern with politics."

He encouraged the clergy to instead attend to their pastoral duties with greater concern. The lower clergy should be loyal to the Apostolic Church, not to the establishment or the conservative party. This would help to restore the lost support of the middle and lower classes for the Church, not in dependency on the aristocracy. The role of the bishops is to provide for the spiritual well-being of their flocks, but the political defense of the Church was the function of the laity. The sermon, "National Apostasy," was the perfect manifesto of principles that would be taken up by the Oxford Movement and in "Tracts for the Times," also known as Tractarianism.

In a sense, Newman went one step beyond Keble. Newman believed that the spiritual function of the Church was "corrupted" by the union of Church and state, and that the Church would be better off without the alliance. Newman had an antipathy to religious liberalism, that doctrine was no more than a matter of opinion. Within the government, every sort of clergyman was eligible for a bishopric. Newman, in a Tract for the Times, wrote that "I wish to encourage Churchmen to look at the possibility of the Church being made to dwell in the affections of the people at large. At present it is too much a Church of the aristocracy, and the poor, through the aristocracy."

Newman admitted that "I cannot love the 'Church of England' commonly so designated (its very title is an offense) for it implies that it is not the Church Catholic but of the state. . . . Viewed internally it is a battle field of two opposite principles: Socinianism and Catholicism."[5]

Published "Tracts of the Times" were written anonymously and distributed by Newman and his friends riding horseback from parsonage to parsonage. The pamphlets spread far and wide and became the source of discussion, gatherings, dinners, and much correspondence.

Tract 1 was addressed to the clergy and authored by Newman, who wrote many of them. The state of the clergy at the time was sad. More than half resided outside their parishes, in better neighborhoods. They hardly ever visited their parishioners. Bishops as well, for the most part, were indolent and wealthy.

In it, Newman wrote, "I am but one of yourselves, a presbyter; and therefore I conceal my name, lest I should take too much on myself by speaking in my own person. Yet speak I must; for the times are evil, yet no one speaks against them. . . . Should the government and the country so far forget their God as to cast off the Church, to deprive it of its temporal honors and substance, on what will you rest the claim of respect and attention which you make upon your flocks? Hitherto you have been upheld by your birth and education, your wealth and your connections; should these secular advantages cease, on what must Christ's ministers depend?"

As Michael Rear assessed the situation, "although there certainly were some devout and industrious clergy, particularly among the Evangelicals, the abuses of pluralism, non-residence, nepotism and sinecures had all flourished almost without interruption since before the Reformation."[6]

It was left to the Oxford Movement to confront the situation and raise the spiritual vision of the clergy.

The Oxford Movement was to take full possession of Newman for the next eight years. At age thirty-two, he was its leader. It was as though the fever he had suffered on his Mediterranean voyage had burned all the past out of him and now he was energized for the future. The Oxford Movement became the battle with the liberal oppression of the Church.

The Parliamentary Reform Bill of 1832, which suppressed ten inactive Anglican dioceses and a few bishoprics in Ireland, is a significant event which Newman saw as the first step in the secularization of the Church by the state. Not only did it give birth to the Oxford Movement, but the Oxford Movement experience would eventually lead Newman into the Catholic Church.

Tract 90, published nine years later in 1841, caused so much controversy, it spelled the end of the "Tracts of the Times." In it Newman asserted that the thirty-nine articles of the Church of England are not contrary to Roman Catholic doctrine. They were, he insisted, aimed instead at corrupt Roman practices and thus were capable of a Catholic interpretation—not at variance with the Council of Trent.

Protestant England rose up in a rage. The heads of the colleges at Oxford declared the tract was incompatible with Oxford University statutes. Newman's university career was ended. The bishops of Oxford banned all future tracts. Newman was denounced as a traitor everywhere. He retired to Littlemore, where he had a small mission parish, St. Mary and St. Nicholas, with a small band of followers.

On September 25, 1843, some eighteen months later, Newman preached his last sermon at St. Mary's University Church, "The Parting of Friends." He then took off his hood and draped on the rail, a sign that he was no longer a teacher in the Church of England. The scene at St. Mary's the following Sunday was compared to "the silence in a cathedral, when the great bell, tolling overhead, had suddenly gone still."

Newman had been vicar of St. Mary's near Oriel College for fifteen years. Newman wrote, "It was at Oxford and by parochial sermons (St. Mary's) that I gained my influence."[7] His first sermon was preached in St. Mary's in 1828, at the age of twenty-seven, and his last sermon, no. 604, September 25, 1843, at the age of forty-two.

As vicar of St. Mary's Newman visited the sick and instructed children and provided Evensong. Eventually, the attendance at his Sunday sermons began to increase to as many as five hundred. Lord Coleridge wrote, "There was scarcely a man of note in the university, young or old, who did not during the last two or three years of Newman's incumbency habitually attend the service and listen to the sermons."[8]

For the first forty-four years of his life, Newman belonged to London and to Oxford. He was a Londoner by birth. The London Stock Exchange building, which stands where Newman was born, has a plaque on the front to his memory, as does the house on Southampton Place, where Newman lived at the time he enrolled in Oxford.

The Academy of Ealing, where Newman attended prep school, no longer stands, but the house in the village of Ham, where Newman spent many happy hours as a youth, still stands and has been appropriately marked. It is a public building today, but the large sycamore where Newman played as a boy still ages.

Littlemore

The hamlet of Littlemore, on the fringe of Newman's parish at St. Mary's University Church, became at once a challenge, a duty, and a rest. He administered the needs of each of his parishioners in Littlemore as well. For eighteen years, almost from the day he took possession of St. Mary's Church in Oxford as vicar, Newman made the three-mile trip to and from Littlemore usually on foot many times a week.

Newman early on decided Littlemore needed its own chapel, so that St. Mary's and Littlemore could become separate parishes. But he had to wait several years to achieve this. On September 22, 1836, the Chapel of St. Mary and St. Nicholas was consecrated in Littlemore, with much help from his mother Jemima. When the church was ready for consecration, Mrs. Newman died.

When Bloxam, the curate of Littlemore resigned in 1840, Newman decided to move to Littlemore. He was drawn to it and also felt by then less at home in Oxford. It was then he began to think of a quasi-monastery at Littlemore, shall we say, already the Oratory, for theological students. He even began designing a building.

In January 1942, Newman wrote, "I have taken a lease of the cottages in Littlemore." He was again thinking about a theological college. The cottages recently had been a stable. The barn would become a library and the cottages would become cells. Interestingly, today it is called the College. Oxford knew it as a monastery.

On April 19, 1842, Newman opened the doors to students.

According to Newman's biographer, Merial Trevor, "Newman did not choose those who came; they were young men made restless in the search for a Catholic life—some refused positions because of their views, others sent by their families in the hope that Newman would persuade them not to 'go over to Rome.' The Littlemore community was never an attempt at a monastic order."[9]

Newman and his followers continued to live at Littlemore in the refurbished horse barns in prayer and study, as he worked translating the treatise of St. Anthanasius against Arius.

Thus, Littlemore was more of a part of Newman's journey of faith than merely a place where he was received into the Catholic Church just before midnight on October 1, 1845 by Passionist Father Dominic Barberi.

After more than four years of spiritual and intellectual struggles at Littlemore, Newman came to reject the Branch Theory, by which the Tractarians had maintained that the Catholic Church had divided into three branches: Roman, Orthodox, and Anglican. Newman now believed in the unity of the Church.

Michael Rear, in a booklet on Newman published on the 150th anniversary of the Oxford Movement, wrote, "For Newman now, the Church had no branches. All antiquity bore witness to the unity of the Church. Modern Roman doctrines were legitimate developments, granted the assumption that divine providence was guiding the Church, giving it the capacity for renewal."

And so Newman would argue, as he began to write at this time his *Essay on the Development of Doctrine*, which would resolve his doubts that the Catholic Church had added to the revealed truth found in antiquity.

Before he finished the essay Newman was received into the Catholic Church. His ideas in the *Essay on Development* would later be assimilated into the *Dogmatic Constitution on Divine Revelation* of the Second Vatican Council, more that 120 years later.

Littlemore was three miles away and was unaffected by the affairs at Oxford. All the simple folks of Littlemore cared about was that their vicar Newman was still at home ministering to them. The College continued to bustle, as students came and went. Newman was now at work writing his *Essay on the Development of Doctrine*, in which his twenty years of study of the Fathers of the Church led him to discover the spirit of the early apostolic Church.

In the words of the late Bernard Basset, S.J., a Newman scholar, "Alone in his cold room, day after day, standing at his writing desk, he worked through century after century, starting with the development of ideas, distinguishing between valid growth and contrary corruptions, so many of which he had charged against the Church of Rome. Papal supremacy, purgatory, mariolatry, the cult of the saints are tested in turn. Beyond each historical research lie the greater concept of the development of doctrine as a whole. . . . John Henry's sense of the development of doctrine is now unwittingly accepted through the Christian world."

The preface of his *Essay on the Development of Doctrine*, incidentally, ends, "Littlemore, October 6, 1845."

On October 8, John Henry Newman posted a letter to a friend, which reads:

"My Dear Mrs. Bowden,

"I am this night expecting Father Dominic, the Passionist, on his way from Aston to Staffordshire to Belgium, where he goes to attend the chapter of his order, and he, please God, will admit me tomorrow or Friday into what I believe to be the one true fold of Christ.

"I have seen the Padre once, on St. John the Baptist's day last year, when I showed him the chapel here. He was a poor boy, who I believe kept sheep near Rome, and from his youth his thoughts have been most singularly and distinctly turned to the conversion of England. He is a shrewd, clever man, but as unaffected and simple as a child and most singularly kind in his thoughts of religious persons of our Communion. I wish all persons were as charitable as I know him to be. After waiting nearly thirty years, suddenly his superiors sent him to England without any act of his own. However, he has not labored in conversions, but confined himself to missions and retreats among his own people. I believe him to be a very holy man.

"I have so many letters to write that I must break off. I shall not send this until it is all over.

"John Henry Newman"

Today, the stables, converted into a "college" by Newman at Littlemore, are owned by the Birmingham Oratory, and they have been restored. The international

33

community, "The Work," which has Newman centers in Italy, Austria and Israel, has taken over the direction of the center at Littlemore.

Conversion

After Newman was received into the Church, he attended Mass at St. Clement's Church, Oxford, (since replaced by a beautiful Jesuit St. Aloysius Church) where Newman returned, after receiving the cardinalate at age seventy-eight, to preach two final sermons. It was a thrilling experience for the aged Newman to return to Oxford.

On October 9, 1845, at Littlemore, John Henry Newman was received into the Catholic Church by Dominick Barberi, the Passionist priest and itinerant apostle to England, since then beatified. Newman had come to believe in the "one and only fold of the Redeemer."

Hundreds of university and educated men, women, priests and laity, followed Newman into the Catholic Church. His Anglican friend and co-worker in the Oxford Movement, Pusey, would write, "Our Church has not known how to employ him. And since this was so, it seemed to me as if a sharp sword were lying on the scabbard. . . . He seems to me not so much gone from us, as transplanted into another part of the vineyard, where the full energies of his powerful mind can be employed."[10]

It was the same John Henry Newman who had captivated the students at Oriel College, Oxford, and with his Sunday sermons at St. Mary's Church. He and his friends were trying to call the Church of England to a renewed sense of Holiness and Christian integrity. Students thronged each Sunday to hear the gentle, ascetic, profound thinker preach.

It was the search for an authentic, politically independent Church that led the scholarly Newman to study the early Fathers of the Church and to search the scriptures. His search led dramatically to his conversion, more than 140 years ago. It was a conversion that has had an enormous impact on both the Church of England and the Catholic Church until this very day.

Newman's conversion meant a painful separation of Anglican friends and collaborators, and an entrance into a Catholic Church he had not known and was slow to accept him. It was not until he was seventy-eight years old that a newly elected pope, Leo XIII, lifted the cloud from Newman's Catholic years by naming him a cardinal of the Church.

Newman's conversion was a process rather than a sudden decision which led him into the Catholic Church. While a dramatic event for the Anglican Church, as well as the Catholic Church, for Newman it marked no dramatic change in his life. "I was not conscious to myself," he wrote, "on my conversion of any change, intellectual or moral, wrought in my mind. I was not conscious of a firmer faith in the fundamental truths of revelation, or of more self-command; I had no more fervor; but it was like coming into port after a rough sea." He simply accepted one more loving invitation from God.

Newman's conversion seems to have been an ongoing struggle between his feelings and his intellect. He had always been sensitive to the interaction between the imagination and the rational mind. His major work, *The*

Grammar of Assent, published in 1879, when he was sixty-eight years old, would deal with this interaction. As is often the case, either reason later catches up with the imagination, or the imagination may never keep up with the intellect's progress.

Early on, at his first conversion in 1816, at age fifteen, Newman had become convinced that the pope was the anti-Christ predicted by the prophet Daniel, St. Paul, and St. John. He records that his "imagination was stained by this doctrine up to the year 1843,"[11] or two years before his conversion to Catholicism. As a youth he had been deeply impressed by anti-popery. Only in time did his imagination become less anti-papal than his intellect.

But it was during his Mediterranean voyage that Newman's imagination was first impressed, in Catholic countries. He writes, "the sight of so many great places, venerable shrines and noble churches much impressed my imagination."[12]

So also was his heart touched. Again, he wrote home, "and my heart was touched also. Making an expedition on foot across some wild country in Sicily, at six in the morning, I came across a small church. I heard voices, and looked in. It was crowded, and the congregation was singing. Of course, it was the Mass, though I did not know it at the time. And in my weary days in Palermo, I was not ungrateful for the comfort which I received in frequenting the churches, nor did I ever forget it. . . . Thus I learned to have tender feelings toward her [the Church of Rome], but still my reason was not affected at all. My judgment was against her, when viewed as an institution, as truly as it ever had been."[13]

Ian Ker, noted Newman scholar and biographer, explored the impact of Newman's Mediterranean tour on his conversion. Ker believes that the crucial month abroad before the commencement of the Oxford Movement, when Newman had first-hand experienced Catholicism, had a profound effect on his eventual conversion in 1845. He bases his view on letters now available which Newman wrote home while abroad.

Ker says, "it is not surprising that a reader of the *Apologia* might well think that Newman's deconversion from Anglicanism really began in that fateful long summer. But what the travel letters of 1821-23 show so graphically is that the imaginative seeds of Newman's eventual conversion to Rome were sown during his visits to the countries of Southern Europe, where there existed two forms of Christianity which had never been 'reformed' by the Reformation and which could reach their origin directly and uninterruptedly back to the early primitive Church of the apostles and martyrs."[14]

He refers, of course, to Roman Catholics and Eastern Orthodoxy, both of which Newman experienced during his travels. He was impressed by both.

Newman had always considered the Greek Fathers as his mentor, particularly, St. Athanasius. He thus could also write to his mother that he found everything in the Roman Catholic cathedral admirable, albeit "a beautiful flower run to seed." The perversions of the Catholic Church still obsessed him, so much that one day he would characterize corruption almost as a note of the Church.

Despite these experiences, Newman still believed the pope to be the anti-Christ. His feelings about Roman Catholicism remained mingled, which almost paralyzed him. He wrote, "You are in the place of martyrdom and burial of the apostles and saints—you have about you buildings and sights they saw—and you are the city to which England owes the blessing of the gospel—But then on the other hand the superstitions;—or rather, what is far worse, the solemn reception of them as an essential part of Christianity—but then again, the extreme beauty and costliness of the churches—and then on the contrary the knowledge that the most famous was built (in part) by the sale of indulgences—really, this is a cruel place. There is more and more to be seen and thought of daily—it is a mine of all sorts of excellences, but the very highest."[15]

Ker concludes there is no doubt that "his religion had been dramatically widened, and there is no question that his imagination, if not his intellect, had been powerfully affected by witnessing first hand the Church which his early evangelical formation had convinced him was the Church of the anti-Christ."[16]

Newman was clearly perplexed by the Church of Rome. "I cannot quite divest myself of the notion that Rome Christian is somehow under an especial shade as Rome Pagan certainly was—though I have seen nothing here to confirm it. Not that one can tolerate for an instant the wretched perversion of the truth which is sanctioned here, but I do not see my way enough to say that there is anything peculiar in the condition of Rome."[17]

Nonetheless, Newman felt his fundamental objection to Rome had not changed. "A union with Rome, while it is what it is, is impossible; it is a dream. As to the individual members of the cruel Church, who can but love and feel for them? I am sure I have seen persons in Rome, who thus move me, though they cast out our name as evil. There is so much amiableness and gentleness, so much oxonianism (so they say), such an amusing and interesting demureness, and such a simplicity of look and speech, that I feel for those indeed who are bound with an iron chain, which cripples their energies, and (one would think) makes their devotion languid. What a strange situation it is, to be with those who think one in a state of perdition, who speak calmly with one, while they have awful thoughts! What a mixture of grief and indignation, what a perplexity between frankness and reserve come over me."[18]

Newman would pen:

Oh that thy creed were sound!
for thou dost soothe the heart, the church of Rome,
By the unwearied watch and varied round
of service, in thy Savior's holy home.[19]

It would take the Oxford Movement to bring Newman's intellect in sinc with his imagination.

Newman was called to Catholicism through a "kindly light" and through the exterior events of his life as an Anglican, in particular the Oxford Movement and his co-worker and friend, Richard Hurrell Froude, whose influence helped Newman "shed some of his evangelical prejudices against Rome, acquire a sense of reverence for the Blessed Virgin Mary and gradually to come to believe in the Real Presence of Christ in the eucharist."[20]

Newman wrote, "When someone comes to God to be saved, then, I say, the essence of true conversion is a surrender of self, an unreserved, unconditional surrender; and this is a saying most who come to God cannot receive. They wish to be saved but in their own way.

"And this is the true Christian state, and the nearest approach to Christ's calm and placid sleep in the tempest; not perfect joy and certainty in heaven, but a deep resignation to God's will, surrender of ourselves, soul and body, to him, hoping indeed that we shall be saved, but fixing our eyes more earnestly on him and ourselves.

"Faith at most only makes us a hero, but love makes a saint."[21]

Chapter Two

Newman's Catholic Years in Birmingham

It was painful enough for John Henry Newman, at midpoint in his life, to part with his Anglican friends at Oxford University to become a Catholic. It became just as painful personally not readily to be accepted by the Roman Catholic Church, which knew very little of him and viewed him with suspicion.

Much of his Catholic years centered in controversy, until at age seventy-eight Newman was completely vindicated when Pope Leo XIII, in one of his first actions as pope, named him a cardinal of the Church. The pillar of the cloud had been lifted from him, he observed.

As a Catholic he had a few run-ins with prelates and priests in England, Ireland and Rome. To find a central point in all these differences of viewpoint, it might be fair to say Newman was not an ultramontane kind of Catholic.

His faith had deep roots in his Anglican heritage and in an intense study of the Fathers of the early Church and scripture. He never rejected his religious heritage when he became a Catholic, as many converts of his day did.

When he had theological reservations about the doctrine of papal infallibility, debated during the First Vatican Council (1869-70), once the doctrine was defined, Newman accepted it wholeheartedly.

Soon after his reception into the Catholic Church at Littlemore, Newman began his preparations for the priesthood at Collegio Propaganda Fide in Rome, but not before he moved his band of followers from Littlemore to Maryville, at Oscott College seminary, at the request of Bishop Nicholas Wiseman. Bishop Wiseman, the first bishop of Birmingham, gave them a home, Maryvale, to live in.

Within a year Newman and his followers went their separate ways to study for the priesthood. Newman and Ambrose St. John early in 1846 set off to study theology in Rome. Although the academic standards at the College of Propaganda Fide in Rome were not as high as Oxford University, Newman fell in love with Rome with its sense of history, churches, fountains and architecture.

The Idea of an Oratory

In Rome, Newman's major problem was to settle his vocation and that of the small group who wished to throw their lot with him. He considered various religious orders and settled on the Oratorians founded in the sixteenth century in Rome, not a new order, but a group of secular priests who lived together without taking vows and with "no bond but that of love." Each house at the Oratory lived its own separate democratic life, and must be situated with a church in a town. From there its influence was to radiate, by its service and preaching, study and learned work.

Newman was immediately attracted by St. Philip Neri,

who had founded the Oratory. He later would describe him, "He would be but an ordinary individual priest as others: and his weapons should be but unaffected humility and unpretending love. All he did was to be done by the light, and fervor, and convincing eloquence of his personal character and his easy conversation."

To his sister Jemima, Newman wrote, "This great saint reminds me in so many ways of Keble, that I can fancy what Keble would have been, if God's will had been that he should have been born in another place or age; he was formed in the same type of extreme hatred of humbug, playfulness, nay oddity, tender love for others, and serenity, which are the lineaments of Keble."[1]

At the time of his conversion, Newman at age forty-four was facing the second half of his life. He was in search of a lifestyle as a Catholic that would allow him to be "a continuation of his former self," not as becoming a "sort of instrument of others, and so clearly beginning life again."[2]

It took him a year and a half to decide on the Oratory, an idea that came originally from his bishop, Nicholas Wiseman, then in Birmingham. In making his choice, Newman was as much concerned about his followers as for himself. (They were now at Maryvale.) The Jesuits, the Dominicans, the Vincentians, and the Redemptorists—all of these in the end were rejected.

Finally, in consideration of what was practically best for himself as well as for his friends, early in 1847, Newman got a hold of the idea of the Oratory, rather than any model. He was thus able to introduce the idea into English Catholic life, "without any direct supervision, direction, support or backing from Italy."[3]

Monsignor Anthony Stark, former vice-postulator for Newman's Cause, wrote "that Newman's Oratory was thoroughly English from the first and the Birmingham Oratory had continued to be so. The different tone taken on by the London Oratory came about after it separated from Newman."[4]

Once Newman had decided upon the Oratory idea, he bent his energies toward carrying it out. Upon his return from Rome after ordination as a Catholic priest, Newman began his English foundation at Maryvale outside of Birmingham, on a temporary basis, until he could find a more suitable place in the heart of Birmingham.

The heady days when he was a national figure in England through his leadership of the Oxford Movement, as an Anglican, then as a convert, gave way to a new and noiseless life as a pastor of a parish among the poor in Birmingham.

The Birmingham Oratory, which Newman was to found on his return, would be Newman's home the rest of his life. And the establishment of the Oratory would become his major preoccupation upon his return. It would be complicated by the joining of Faber and the seventeen members of a community already established.

Newman had just arrived in England, and while he had five newly ordained priests, with two to come, along with several lay brothers, his Birmingham Oratory was not yet organized.

Newman welcomed Faber and his group, but cautioned, "I will but say that, from the very wish I have that we may come to an understanding, I am anxious you should try it if you have fully mastered what Oratorianism is. In many important aspects it differs from what you are at present. It is not near so ascetic—indeed it is not ascetic. It is not poetical—it is not very devotional. Now it is a question what your youths will say to this. Again, as you know, it has but a few lay brothers compared to your present society. An Oratorian ought, like a Roman legionary, to stand in his place and fight by himself though in company—instead of being a mere instrument of another, or a member of a phalanx. I am so desirous of our coming together, that I wince while I put down these objections, but no good will come of it, if we don't consider the matter in all its bearings."[5]

The acceptance of Faber and his seventeen young men into the Oratory would cause Newman many problems. The young members had no pastoral experience, had not experienced community, and lacked common sense, if not ideals.

Added to this the Oratory had still to find a permanent home in Birmingham, having started out at Maryvale (Oscott), then moved to St. Wilfrid's, which was Faber's community base. From St. Wilfrid's Newman finally brought his community to Birmingham to establish a make-shift home in an old gin distillery on Alcester Street. The date was June 26, 1849, a little more than a year since the Oratory arrived in England.

The work was begun, unexpectedly among a flood of children who came for instruction. A solid Catholic community was established and continues to flourish long after the Oratory made its final move to Edgbastion in 1852, where it is still flourishing today.

From the beginning, Newman had his heart set on London as the home of his Oratory, but in the end, because of his respect for Bishop Ullathorne, the new bishop of Birmingham, who had helped him settle his Oratory in Birmingham, he decided to stay put with the Birmingham Oratory. It would be Faber whom Newman would send to London to head a London Oratory. And so the two Oratories exist yet today in Birmingham and London, but started by Newman, each still bearing the distinctive marks of their original superiors, Father Newman and Father Faber.

Apart from establishing his own unique Oratory in Birmingham, Newman had his hands full with Faber's inconsistencies and eccentricities. From 1845 until 1854, Newman had enough on his plate simply dealing with the internal problems of his two fledging Oratories.

To begin with, Newman had different ideas on what an Oratory should be. He did not slavishly follow the Rule of St. Philip, but tried to adapt it to life in nineteenth century England. Newman from the very beginning was attracted by the idea of an Oratory being a loose association of men working together for God as friends in one particular house. Newman was not by nature disposed to being a "superior," one who would impose rules or order from above. Faber was just the opposite. He would not tolerate any challenge to his authority, and to the end, Meriol Trevor writes, treated his novices and priests as "a sentimental autocrat, alternately punishing and embracing."[6]

The Faber followers were converts full of fervor, more Catholic than the pope, more Roman than the Romans. By virtue of their personalities, Newman and Faber continued their love-hate relationship until the end.

Unlike secular priests, or even order priests Oratorians are a congregation. They enter an Oratory to stay and work in the same place all their life, not subject to being moved around. Each Oratory is self-governing and independent of all the others. If it is a parish, it is subject to the local bishop in parochial matters, and of course, is directly subject to the Holy See.

So it was in Birmingham, where Newman's life as an Oratorian settled into pastoral work—Masses, confessions, visits to the sick, looking after children in the Poor School, and people in the Work House and prison. When this was done, Newman still found time to pursue his own intellectual and journalistic apostolate. He wrote letters, sermons, books, articles, and engaged in the religious controversies of his day.

The Achilli's Trial

This was his life now as a Catholic. Soon, in 1850 to be exact, another issue confronted Newman which, in retrospect, he had best left alone.

But it was a heady time for Catholics in England, when the Catholic hierarchy was restored. Bishop Wiseman was named a cardinal, the first Archbishop of Westminster. For the rest of England, it was a time of fear of popery, that the Catholic Church would take over the country, the Inquisition would be started anew, the pope would rule England. (How history repeats itself.)

Of course Newman and the Oratories were criticized in the press. "No popery. Down with the Oratorians. No religion at all." So all the placards read in demonstrations in London. Newman tried to allay the fears of his countrymen with a series of public lectures in the Birmingham Corn Exchange.

When a former Dominican, an Italian named Achilli, came to England with anti-Catholic horror stories, Newman had enough. He launched out against Achilli in the Corn Exchange, citing certain facts from Cardinal Wiseman's article in the Dublin Review.

It was a mistake. Newman was sued for libel and went into a long drawn out court ordeal. When at last the trial took place, Newman lost, despite massive evidence against Achilli. It was a miscarriage of justice. Achilli disappeared, but Newman had to suffer the indignation.

In the end, he did not have to go to jail, but he did have to pay a heavy fine. The ordeal was a time of humiliation that took its toll on him.

The Second Spring

To soothe him, Cardinal Wiseman invited him to preach before the assembly of the new Catholic bishops, meeting in Synod, in Oscott, in July 1852.

His famous sermon, "The Second Spring," on the restoration of the hierarchy in England and the return of the Catholic faith in England, has been recognized as beautiful, powerful and literary as any he had preached, and it remains a classic in the English language. In the audience that memorable day was Henry Edward Manning, who would became the next archbishop of Westminster and Newman's greatest critic.

Cardinal Wiseman's biographer, Ward, describes the occasion. "Still under the shadow of persecution, the rulers of the English Catholic Church assembled at Oscott . . . and once more carried out the full legislative ceremonial of the Church, discussed since the Reformation. . . . At the opening of the second session on July 13, Newman preached the sermon on the Second Spring. As the Mass of the Holy Spirit was celebrated with the music and liturgy in the best Oscott tradition, to ask for light in the deliberations of the first synod of the new hierarchy—the Church largely filled with the children of the Oxford Movement, Manning, Oakeley, Faber, and others, the great Oxford descendants of the English martyrs—all Wiseman's dreams appeared to be fulfilled. The Cardinal's tears fell fast, so Bishop Ullathorne has told us, while Newman sketched the picture of the glories of the ancient Catholic Church of England; of its death; of the second life which was beginning.

"Newman was overwhelmed by the display of strong feelings he had evoked by his sermon, and was rescued by Henry Edward Manning—then a convert of but one year's standing—from the greetings of enthusiasm with which he was received after the Mass was over."[7]

The Second Spring marks a high point in literature as well. "The past has returned, the dead lives. . . . The English Church was and the English Church was not, and the English Church is once again. This is the portent worthy of a cry. It is the coming of a Second Spring."

Newman was meditating on the winter that overtakes each of us and all we do; but beyond is a vision of a second temple rising above the ruins of the old.

Nearly 150 years have passed since Newman preached the Second Spring.[8] He pointed to the material world around us as an example of the cycle of life and death. "The sun sinks to rise again; the day is swallowed up in the gloom of night, to be born out of it, as fresh as if it had never been quenched. Spring passes into Summer and Autumn into Winter, only by its own return to triumph over the grave, toward which it hastened from the first hour."

"Man rises to fall. He was young, he is old, he is never young again. He is born to die. The noblest efforts of our genius, the conquests we have made, the nation we have civilized outlive us, but in the end tend to dissolution. Mankind and all his works are mortal. They die."

"Not so the Church," Newman says, born from the very side of Christ Easter Sunday. "For the Church the past returns; the dead live. It is the coming of the Second Spring. For the Church, there is death but always new life, as is it for the Christian. Yesterday we were dead. Today we are alive. Because of the death and resurrection of Jesus, the Church constantly renews us and through us renews itself."

The world grows old, but the Church is ever young. "Arise, Jerusalem, for thy light is come, and the glory of the Lord is risen upon thee. Behold, darkness shall cover the earth and a mist the people; but the Lord shall rise upon thee. Arise, make haste my love, my beautiful one, and come. For the Winter is now past. The vines in flower yield their sweet smell."

"One thing I know," Newman concluded his sermon, "that according to our need, so will be our strength."

The Idea of a University

In his efforts to establish a Catholic University in Dublin, a project that engaged him for a good part of the 1850s, John Henry Newman made fifty-six crossings of St. George's Channel from England to Ireland "in the service of the university." One of Newman's major difficulties at this time was leading two lives, one as rector in Dublin, the other as superior of the Oratory in Birmingham. Back and forth he went, and it drained his physical energies.

In the end, the Catholic University project in Dublin was abandoned, and Newman again felt a sense of failure. It seemed the lot of Newman to be associated with projects which during his lifetime were doomed to failure, bringing to him little consolation, but which one hundred years after his death still bear fruit. Today University College Dublin is the largest university in Ireland. It dates its origin from the foundation of the Catholic University of Ireland in 1851. Its doors opened in 1854.

But it was not the best of times to undertake a Catholic University in Ireland, as Newman envisioned it. By way of background, Trinity College Dublin, which was Anglican, established in 1592 by a charter given by Elizabeth I, for two and half centuries was the only university in Ireland. Religious tests were imposed on students and faculty alike.

Then, following the development of religious freedom in Ireland in the early nineteenth century, both Roman Catholics and Protestant dissenters looked for equality of treatment. Intended as a conciliatory measure, Sir Robert Peel in 1845 established the Queen's Colleges in Belfast, Cork and Galway for those Catholics or other dissenters who were unwilling to attend Trinity. These non-denominational colleges, condemned by the Roman Catholic hierarchy in Ireland, led to a decision in 1850 to establish in Ireland a Catholic University, modeled after Louvain University. And Newman shortly thereafter was invited to be the first rector.

Until 1858 he was frustrated, despite his greatest hope to make the university work. Only a handful of fellow converts and friends in Britain followed Newman to Dublin. Instead, the university became an institution for Irish Catholics. At this time, it must be remembered that Archbishop Paul Cullen, who returned to Ireland in 1850 as apostolic delegate and had already spent thirty years of his life in Rome, was the controlling force. His training in Rome as a Roman Catholic and that of Newman as a recent convert from Anglicanism were in sharp contrast. They were temperamentally incompatible.

In post-famine Ireland, the university was hardly a priority among bishops. In effect, there were no qualified students coming from the very few secondary schools. Its degrees were not recognized by the state, nor did it receive state funding. The Irish masses, recovering from the disasters of the famine, had little interest in a Catholic University.

The University Church, which Newman built on Stephen's Green, was the first phase of a Catholic University undertaken by Newman in 1850 at the request of the Irish bishops, on the advice of Pope Pius IX.

After seven years of struggles as the rector, and as he commuted between Birmingham and Dublin, while at the same time establishing his Oratory in Birmingham, Newman resigned as rector. The University Church, which Newman had built "because he wanted to establish from the very outset the union between religion and philosophy," is still a parish church.

The university experienced a rebirth soon after Newman's death in 1890 and thrives today as the University College Dublin, still very much imbued with his spirit.

The Dublin experience gave birth to Newman's classic work, *The Idea of a University*, delivered in part in discourses in 1852. The Catholic University's medical school, also established by Newman, has had a continuous existence and growth since Newman's time.

The story of this remarkable institution begins with John Henry Newman. Today there are two memorials of the seven years during which Newman lived off and on in Dublin—a bust of Newman in the University Church, on St. Stephen's Green, and a modest inscription, Newman House, on the railings of the house next door.

From the beginning, John Henry Newman saw the task as a temporary one. His heart was in Birmingham, with the Oratory. Apart from his first love, the absence of a charter giving public recognition to the degrees of the university, lack of public support, financial difficulties, and some personal difference with Archbishop Cullen all contributed to his discouragement.

The university floundered until 1879, when St. Patrick's House of the Catholic University of Ireland became the University College Dublin. In 1883 the Jesuits took charge, and in 1890, by royal charter, University College Dublin was established. The medical college, established by Newman himself, was incorporated in the University College Dublin (it had been a separate entity), and today it is the largest medical college in Ireland.

Today, there are two major universities in Ireland—Trinity College and University College Dublin. Founded in 1592 as a Protestant University, Trinity College did not admit Catholics until 1793, and not until 1873 were all religious tests eliminated. Thus the need for a Catholic University, to which Newman responded.

John Newman was invited to meet the challenge. Despite the fact that the Catholic University of Ireland, founded by Newman, received no monies from the state and was supported only by donations of the Irish Catholic poor, and its degrees were not recognized, apart from the medical degrees, and student enrollment was small, yet Newman was not discouraged. "I see," he said later, "a flourishing university, which for a while had to struggle with fortune, but which, when its founders and servants were dead and gone, had successes far exceeding their anxieties."[9] Prophetic words indeed.

It was Newman's idea that the supreme function of a university is to develop personal intelligence through the pursuit of knowledge for its own sake. For Newman, "the object of a Catholic University is to reunite what has been put asunder," without stunting growth or compromising freedom in either the intellectual or the religious discipline. "What I am stipulating for is, that they should be found in one and the same place, and exemplified in the same person."[10]

Newman early on sensed the Irish bishops were not behind the venture. Cardinal Wiseman of Westminster indicated to Newman he would be named a bishop to enhance his role as rector, but when the document came from Rome appointing him rector of the Dublin Catholic University, no mention of bishop was made.

The Irish bishops never told Newman they didn't want a university, but continued to fuss about finances. The discipline of the university, and its liberal ideas, and Newman's hiring of lay faculty to train Irish youths irritated them. When Newman finally realized neither he nor his university were welcome in Dublin, he resigned.

"It was not Ireland, or the Irish people who were unkind to me," he said. "The same thing would have happened in England or France. It was the clergy."[11]

Newman's discourses on *The Idea of a University* live on. It was *The Idea of a University* and Newman's later aborted attempts to establish a Catholic College at Oxford University that inspired the Newman Movement on secular campuses in the United States. Today, better known as Campus Ministry, the Newman movement continues to show a new vitality.

Upon his return to England in 1858 Newman carried on his work at the Oratory, preaching weekly homilies, writing books and letters, and engaging in religious controversies of the day. He founded the Oratory school in 1859, and he took an active part in the First Vatican Council.

Chapter Three

The Measure of the Catholic Spirit

John Henry Newman was a many-sided personality. Because he was named a cardinal of the Church he is viewed as a great upholder of things Catholic and a polemicist against the Church's detractors. But another side of Newman is less known and appreciated, and that is his advocacy of freedom of thought, his defense of the role of the laity in the Church, and his criticism of authoritarianism in the Church.

In these areas he was in the mainstream of the Second Vatican Council and its thrust toward a more open Church, even though that Council was not to convene until seventy years after Newman's death. Newman had to contend with the First Vatican Council in his day, which confronted the touchy question of infallibility in the Church. He was not on the side of the angels in that heated controversy.

Newman combined those rare qualities, which we still need today, of loyalty to the Church along with questioning. He could both love and criticize the Church. As a public figure in the Church, the tensions between his commitment to the Church and his voice of reform were highlighted.

Newman was critical of a clericalism which did not heed the experience of the laity. He wanted theologians to take into account the *concensus fidelium*. He rejected a static view of truth set once and for all in concrete. For him, all believers formed together a community, and no single segment of it—the clergy, for example—had an exclusive hold on revelation.

"The Church comes to understanding and grows in that understanding with the participation of all its members," as one Newman scholar expressed it. Revelation is a form of dialogue within the Church of many different views and faith experiences.

His appeal for freedom of thought was expressed in these words to his friend Pusey: "Life has the same right to decay, as it has to wax strong. This is specially the case with great ideas. You may stifle them; or you may refuse them elbow room; or again, you may torment them with your continual meddling; or you may let them have free course and range, and be content, instead of anticipating their excesses, to expose and restrain those excesses after they have occurred. But you have only this alternative; and for myself, I prefer much wherever it is possible, to be first generous and then just; to grant full liberty of thought, and to call it to account when abused."

Newman couldn't conceive of a Church cut off from the laity. It would be voiceless. He saw his vocation as an educator and a shaper of public opinion. For this work an educated laity was his colleague. It is the role of the laity to shape the national ethos. He gave this mandate to the laity:

"You might be able to dispense on all sides of you the royal light of truth, and exert an august moral influence upon the world . . . it as a moral force, not a material, which will vindicate your profession and will secure your triumph. It is not giants who do most. . . . I want an intelligent, well-instructed laity. . . . I wish you to enlarge your knowledge, to cultivate your reason, to get an insight into the relation of truth to truth. . . . In all times the laity have been the measure of the Catholic spirit."[1]

For this reason he fought for the unpopular cause of admitting young Catholics to Oxford University, and he felt the laity ought to be consulted on this matter of pastoral practice. Eventually, he was to write a controversial piece, "On Consulting the Faithful in Matters of Doctrine." [-]

Indeed, the lay person has emerged in the renewal of the Church initiated by the Second Vatican Council. Some laity think their progress in the process has been all too slow and circumscribed by clerical authority. Some pastors and bishops feel the laity have become too critical and aggressive. Perhaps a return to Newman can help us yet today in resolving these tensions.

John Henry Newman had a holistic, historical vision of the Church. He saw it as an independent union of papacy, episcopacy, clergy and laity. The conciliar document of Vatican II, *Lumen Gentium*, adopted Cardinal Newman's view of the Church, first of all, as the people of God—"the faithful are consecrated to be a spiritual house and a holy priesthood.

"Though they differ essentially and not only in degree, the common priesthood of the faithful and the ministerial or hierarchical priesthood are more or less ordered one to another; each in its own proper way share in the one priesthood of Christ."

Newman insisted upon the need for an enthusiastic, educated and involved laity within the Church. Father Stephen Dessain, a noted Newman scholar, wrote: "Newman's ideal was an educated laity who understood their faith, so that they could participate in the mission of the Church."[2] *Lumen Gentium* and the *Decree on the Apostolate of Lay People* both reaffirmed this and added the note that lay people also are called to be apostolic.

Newman saw the Catholic University as the via media between the ultras of both sides—the ultra liberals and the ultra conservatives. An extract from one of his letters sums this up. "So far as I can see, there are ecclesiastics all over Europe whose policy is to keep the laity at arms length, and hence, the laity have been disgusted and become infidel, and only two parties exist, both ultras in opposing directions. . . . You will be doing the greatest possible benefit to the Catholic cause all over the world if you succeed in making the university a middle station at which laity and clergy can meet, so as to learn to understand and to yield to each other, and from this, as from a common ground, they may act in union upon an age which is running headlong into infidelity."[3] Words true yet today.

Newman wanted intellectual lay people who were religious at heart, and he wanted a devout clergy who were intellectual. If the faithful are cut off from the study of divine doctrines, he wrote, and simply asked for implicit faith in the Church's word, the educated classes will become indifferent and the poor classes superstitious.

"Christ," for Newman, "is an individual person whose likeness has been implanted in the mind and heart of all the faithful—laity, bishops, religious, priests. It is this holy community that is the whole Church, and the Church continually develops in knowledge and love."[4] So wrote French lay theologian Jean Guitton, who was the only layman invited to the first sessions of the Second Vatican Council by Pope John XXIII.

The Rambler

The Rambler, a Catholic review founded in England in 1848 by friends of John Henry Newman, was an intellectual review. Its editorial goals were to respond to the false intellectualism of the age, defend Catholicism, and present the Catholic viewpoint on discoveries of the age—to bring together the Church and the modern age.

The collaborators on *The Rambler* were Catholic lay persons who considered themselves independent of the ecclesiastical authority when treating lay subjects. The review was more cultural than political. Though it never exceeded eight hundred subscribers, *The Rambler* had considerable influence. One contributor was Lord Acton, a leading English intellectual.

Newman sought to be a conciliator, as he defended *The Rambler* before the bishops, and defended the bishops before the editors of *The Rambler*. True journalist in his own right, Newman defended the Christian past, but was not afraid to engage in the present conflicts. He wanted to meet the modern age, but also regenerate the Church. His instincts were with *The Rambler*.

But once again he had to break with his friends on *The Rambler*. He was ever loyal to religious authority. He sought again a via media. Eventually, in 1859, Newman took the editorship of *The Rambler* at the request of Cardinal Wiseman, when the journal was in troubled waters. At this time there was conflict between the bishops and the Catholic liberals over educational policies.

Newman thought the laity ought to be consulted on the matter, and this got him into deep trouble. To clarify his ideas, Newman wrote a long article in *The Rambler* entitled, "On Consulting the Faithful in Matters of Doctrine." He was misunderstood and surprised at the negative reactions.

Newman had tried to distinguish between the unanimous faith of the Church (as a community) and the power of defining the faith (the province of the hierarchy). He cited the dogma of the Immaculate Conception to illustrate his case—the laity had been consulted. Again, Newman wanted the whole Church involved.

Newman's ideas were finally accepted by the Second Vatican Council. In the *Dogmatic Constitution on the Church*, the Council Fathers said: "The universal body made up of the faithful whom the Holy One has anointed, is incapable of being at fault in belief."

It was Newman who had cited the Arian heresy of the fourth century to show how the faithful had kept the faith at a time when many bishops accepted the heresy. Newman was surprised so many bishops turned Arian, while so many of the laity remained Catholic.

Although Newman's essay "On Consulting the Faithful in Matters of Doctrine" caused an uproar in England and

Rome more than one hundred years ago, today the issue seems to be of minor interest.

The very idea of the hierarchy "consulting the laity" was considered heretical. After an exchange of letters and face-to-face conversations with Bishop Ullathorne, Newman recalled the conversation. "He thought there were remains of old spirit [in *The Rambler*]. It was irritating. Our laity were a peaceable set, the Church was at peace. They had a deep faith—they did not like to hear that anyone doubted. . . . I said in answer that he saw one side, I another—that the bishops, etc., did not see the state of the laity (e.g.) in Ireland—how unsettled yet how docile. He said something like, 'Who are the laity?' I answered that the Church would look foolish without them."[5]

Newman gave up the editorship of *The Rambler*.

Today the word "consult" itself has a dialogical meaning, whereas Newman had a narrow definition—like consulting a dictionary to verify a meaning or taking the pulse of the faithful to find a *sensus fidelium*. This is not a democratic process, but a sensitivity to what the faithful—pastors and laity—believe in their hearts on a given issue. The *sensus fidelium* is like an instinct to sense error as well as to sense the scandal of error.

John Henry Newman has been faulted by some of his critics for not treating the social issues of nineteenth-century England and for not being involved in social activist movements for the rights of workers, prison reform, and other issues rising out of the industrial revolution. It was the same century that produced Dickens, John Stuart Mill, Thomas Hood, and two social actionists who often were at odds with Newman: Charles Kingsley and Cardinal Henry Manning. Yet Newman was silent.

Manning had become involved in prison reform a[nd] in an agrarian revolt to improve housing and wages, and eliminate child labor. He backed the dock workers' strike of 1889.

In retrospect, one hundred years after his death, it now can be seen that Newman's great contribution to issues of justice and peace were in his respect for the role of the laity in the Church. Newman undoubtedly saw the social concerns of the day as the province of an educated, committed, faithful laity, and not the work of clergymen.

As a pastor of the Birmingham Oratory, itself serving the working classes of the industrial city of Birmingham, Newman and his priests personally attended to the poor and the needy in their parish. This was his pastoral approach. "The best preparation for loving the world at large," he wrote, "is to cultivate an intimate friendship and affection toward those who are immediately about us."[6]

Newman believed the laity should be educated in order to prepare them for the world. A university, Newman wrote, is not a convent or a seminary, but a direct preparation for the world. The following stirring appeal to the laity contained in his lectures on "The Present Position of Catholics in England" ring true today.

"What I desiderate in Catholics is the gift of bringing out what their religion is. . . . You must not hide your talents in a napkin, or your light under a bushel. I want a laity, not arrogant, not rash in speech, not disputatious, but who know their religion, who enter into it, who know just where they stand, who know what they hold and what they do not, who know their creed as well, that they can give an account of it; who know so much of history that they can defend it.

"I want an intelligent, well-instructed laity. I am not denying that you are such already, but I mean to be severe, and some would say, exorbitant in my demands; I wish you to enlarge your knowledge, to cultivate your reasons, to get an insight into the relation of truth to truth, to learn to view things as they are, to understand how faith and reason stand to each other who are the bases and principles of Catholicism."[7]

Newman worried that the liberals of his day, who were concerned with temporal issues, were outside the teaching of the Church, and therefore their social conscience was not enlightened by faith.

Newman appealed to the classic definition of conscience as the "voice of God," whereas his nineteenth-century contemporaries appealed to a conscience which had no thought of God at all.

The laity today live in a world in which Church teachings and secular practices are often far apart. We need only to consider respect life issues, war and peace, economic injustices, bio-genetics, civil rights. Newman's response was that the faithful must follow the law of conscience in the classical sense—the voice of God—in considering the issues of the day, enlightened by the teachings of the Church.

It was the view of Newman that while the laity participated in the three-fold office of Christ as priest, king and prophet, the prophetic role was perhaps most clearly the vocation of the laity. Newman discerned that the laity of the Christian world are in the current of prophetism.

In a sermon preached in St. Mary's Church in Oxford,

he developed the classic distinction of the three offices of Christ. The faithful, he says, reproduce Christ. They too are priests, kings and prophets. The lay person is king when he or she works and endures to dominate the earth; priests, through prayer and through suffering. The prophetic role is the Church in action as distinct from the Church quiescent. For Newman, faith is not a static gift, a closed treasure. Rather, it lives in the whole body of believers who labor to make it explicit. Faith is not a special possession of an elite sacerdotal body, but shared by all members of the Church. Each is called to contribute to the fruition of faith by works and by knowledge. The laity have not received the charge to define, to decide magisterially, because that requires an authority, with a charism to preserve it from error. But the laity are the living tradition at work.

Newman always thought the Holy Spirit worked through the Church, almost naively at times, through an instinct of common piety, especially at a time when theologians, following straight logic, could end in error.

It would seem to me that since the end of the Second Vatican Council, when the Council Fathers developed this threefold office of the laity, an emphasis in the Church has been overly placed on the participation of the laity in the priesthood of Christ, and not enough on the more important role of the laity as witnesses, as prophets.

The multiplication of lay ministries, so many of them centered in the sanctuary and as an extension of the ministry of the priesthood has resulted, in the minds of some, in a clericalization of the laity.

In much of the preparatory meetings of the Synod of

Bishops on the Laity, the thrust was to revive the prophetic role of the laity, the role of laity as witnesses in the temporal order—the professions, politics, family, community, workplaces, business, the art and other specifically lay areas of influence.

Newman had great faith in the ordinary men and women in the Church, who, without theology and philosophy, can discover true faith and witness to it. Christ takes possession of Christians, and Christians take possession of Christ.

Giving to the word, "prophet," the full meaning which Newman intended, Jean Guitton, in his remarkable book, *The Church and the Laity*, writes: "The prophet is the person of God, who also attends closely not to the abstract dialect of history so dear to false prophets, but to the real, ever new, never predictable movement of divine and human history. Plunged in time, nourished by its mystery, the prophet considers each day in the light of eternity, that he may strive to utter the truth most needed for the day."[8]

We have come a long way since the days of the last century when the laity's role in the Church was described by Msgr. George Talbot (1867) as "to hunt, to shoot, to entertain. . . . These matters they understood, but to meddle in ecclesiastical matters, they have no rights at all."

Chapter Four

God's Noiseless Work

John Henry Newman never wrote about spirituality as such, nor did he use the term "lay spirituality." Yet there are passages in his sermons and writings that seem apropos to members of the faithful seeking to live in closer union with our Lord. And, of course, in his own personal life there was a strong devotion to the eucharist and Mary, the Mother of Jesus.

Newman certainly did not view the lay person as a kind of mini cleric or a diminished priest. Lay life cannot be patterned after religious life, with holy rules, discipline, dress codes, or vows. Witness the many Secular Institutes or Third Orders, or Opus Dei in the world. But for Newman a lay person is not a religious in the world. The emphasis for the laity must be on the duties of one's state in life. The lay person must be in the world and of the world. The marketplace is where the lay person exercises the prophetic role of teacher and witness.

From Newman's writings, and indeed life, three ideas emerge which can be relevant to a lay spirituality. First of all, there is faith, understood as trusting in the personal guidance of divine providence; then, fidelity, as understood as loyalty to the Church, even in the face of misunderstanding and difficulties; and finally, friendship, understood in the personal relationships with those people who are one's companions in the pilgrimage of faith.

Certitude about faith was essential to Newman, or else how can we pray to a being whose existence we doubt? Without certitude, there can be "no habit of prayer, no directness of devotion, no intercourse with the unseen, no generosity or self-sacrifice."[1] Newman put his trust in the providence of God. "It would be easier for me to believe that there is no God at all, than to think he does not care."[2]

Yet Newman's belief in a divine providence could have been self-centered had it not been balanced with his fidelity to the Church and by his friendships.

Newman based his spiritual life in the "ordinariness" of faith, "a fundamental willingness to place oneself and one's whole career, unconditionally, in the hand of that providence, who is always realized to be kind and full of love, even in one's darkest hour."

Fidelity to the Church was not easy for Newman, for he was often in conflict with ecclesiastical authorities over doctrinal matters.

In all his failures and disappointments, Newman remained steadfast in his opposition of two false ideas of spirituality: one, that stressed religious devotion to the point of disdaining human reason; the other, that stressed ecclesiastical obedience without regard for the contravening circumstances of individual conscience.

Finally, for Newman, friendships revealed that the love of one's neighbor, who we can see, is verification of our love of God, whom we cannot see.

A long-time student of Newman believes he is an

example of a new kind of sanctity peculiar to modern times. Its peculiarity lies in its ordinariness. "It shies away from the miraculous, the extravagant, the external manifestation of mystical experiences," Professor A. J. Boekraad writes. "It performs the task of living a Christian life in the complexity of the modern world well and without ostentation."[3]

What do we mean by "ordinariness"? Certainly not commonplace and easy-going, but a fundamental willingness to place oneself and one's whole career, unconditionally, in the hands of a providence in the most ordinary occurrences of life, because in these ordinary facts God's graces lie hidden. It shows friendliness, goodness and tolerance toward all who are really serious, whatever their age, rank, position, or religious conviction.

Boekraad continues, "It has a liberty and independence of speech, judgment, and criticism, entirely free from bitterness, sarcasm and self-opinionatedness, which can only be due to filial love. Newman's life shows this ideal in the concrete, in his own personality."[4]

Newman was a firm believer in the personal influence of Christians. "Glory, science, knowledge never healed a wounded heart or changed a sinful one," he wrote.[5] But are there enough of such Christians?

"They are enough to carry on God's noiseless work. The apostles were such men; others might be named in their several generations, as successors to their holiness. These communicate their light to a number of less luminaries, by whom, in turn, it is distributed throughout the world. . . . A few highly endowed persons will rescue the world for centuries to come."[6]

Newman always insisted that moral conscience was the voice of God. Whether we have heard the name of the Savior or not, we have within our breast "a certain commanding dictate, not sentiment, not a mere opinion, or impression, or view of things, but a law, an authoritative voice bidding us to do certain things and avoid others."

Newman today has been recognized for his respect for the laity in the Church. He never forgets their concrete situation. "It would be a great mistake for us to suppose we need quit our temporal calling, and go into retirement, in order to serve God acceptably. Christianity is a religion for the world, for the busy and influential as well as for the poor."

For Newman it was a false perspective to feel the next life is all in all and "that eternity is the only subject that really can claim or occupy our thoughts." It is to undervalue this life altogether and to forget its real importance. "The employments of this world though not themselves heavenly are after all the way to heaven, that as Christ is seen in the poor, and in the persecuted and in children, so he is seen in the employments which he puts upon his chosen, whatever they be."

Remarking on St. Paul, Newman writes: "Wonderful to say, he who had rest and peace in the love of Christ, was not satisfied without the love of men. . . . He loved his brethren, not only 'for Jesus' sake,' but for their own sake also." Newman certainly followed his own advice in the friendships he had during his long life.

Truths must be laid up in the heart. "That a thing is true is no reason that it should be said, but that it should be done; that it should be acted upon; that it should be made our own inwardly."

Although John Henry Newman had no special spirituality of his own, he reminds us that "Christianity is eminently an objective religion. For the most part it tells us of persons and facts in simple words, and leaves that announcement to produce its effect on such hearts that are prepared to receive it."

There is in Newman, a balanced doctrine which does not forget the corporate nature of salvation. Coming together for worship is not a mere practical necessity, the rites which convey grace are commuted to the body of Christians. The sacraments, baptism and eucharist, are social and public by their very nature. "It is not that this one receives the blessing and that one, but one and all, the whole body as one person, one new spiritual person, with one accord, seeks and gains it."

The same with prayer. "If Christians are to live together they will pray together; and united prayer is necessarily of an intercessory character, as being offered for each other and for the whole, and for self as one of the whole."

But, of course, the mystical body itself is composed of persons. "Our Lord, by becoming man, has found a way whereby to sanctify that nature of which his own manhood is the pattern specimen. He inhabits us personally, and his inhabitation is effected by the channel of the sacraments." There is an indwelling, a special presence of God in those who are members of our Lord. This truth underlays Newman's lifelong serenity amid so many trials.

In October 1817, at the beginning of the first term at Oxford, he prayed to Almighty God "to give me the Holy Spirit." He was dependent on the Holy Spirit as he was on the air he breathed. "Let us adore the sacred presence within us with all fear and rejoice with trembling. Let us offer up our best gifts to him who, instead of abhorring, has taken up his abode in these sinful hearts of ours."

Newman reminds us we are temples of God. "We are not our own; we are bought with the blood of Christ; we are consecrated to the temples of the Holy Spirit. . . . May we live worthy of our calling."

Since our Lord's return to heaven, we are united to all three divine persons. "We have lost the sensible and unconscious perception of Christ; we cannot look on him, hear him, converse with him, follow him from place to place; but we can enjoy the immaterial, inward, mental, real sight and possession of him; a possession more real and more present than that which the apostles had in the day of his flesh. . . . He enters into us. He claims and takes possession of his purchased inheritance. He makes us his members."

Are you living in the conviction of God's presence, he asks? Do you believe that his light penetrates and shines through your heart? "In all circumstances of joy or sorrow, hope or fear, let us aim at having him in our inmost heart; let us have no secret apart from him."

In this sense the Christian "will be calm and collected under all circumstances; he will make light of injuries and forget them." It is back to invisibility and mystery. "It is in mercy he hides himself from those who would be overcome by the touch of the Almighty hand . . . and though we joy, as well we may, yet we cannot joy with the light hearts of children, who live by sight, but with the thoughtful gladness of grown persons. Where there is liberty from the tyranny of sin, doubt, gloom, impatience have been expelled; joy in the gospel has taken their place. How can charity to men fail?"

For Newman, joy and gladness are the characteristic of the Christian. "Fear is what makes men bigots, tyrants and zealots," but there is a holy fear which makes Christian joy sober and reverent. "Gloom is no Christian temper; the repentance is not real which has not love in it; that self-chastisement is not acceptable, which is not sweetened by faith and cheerfulness.We must live in sunshine, even when in sorrow." He calls this equanimity.

Then, the final prayer for fervor. "Lord, in asking for fervor, I am asking for Thyself, for nothing short of Thee, O my God, who has given Thyself wholly to us. Enter my heart substantially and personally, and fill it with fervor by filling it with Thee. Thou alone canst fill the soul of man, and Thou has promised to do so."

Although Newman loved the Church to the end of his life—"the reason I became a Catholic was because the present Roman Catholic Church is the only Church which is like the primitive Church"—Newman was ever aware of its weaknesses and deficiencies.

He found in the Catholic Church scholastic narrowness, superstition, intrigue and delation. Yet the Church shares in the triple office of Christ as prophet, priest and king. She must give theological teaching, she must worship, and she must govern. Unfortunately, the first tends to rationalism, the second to superstition, and the third to ambition and tyranny.

In his day, he saw exaggerations in the Church—the invocation of the saints, indulgences, the sacrificial aspect of the Mass, the hierarchical nature of the Church, and the juridical aspect, whereas the great truths about the hidden divine element of the Church, the risen Christ and his presence in all believers, were left on one side. There was an imbalance which he tried to correct and which the Second Vatican Council did in fact correct.

Newman's means for reform was personal influence rather than new structures. He preferred the way of a St. Philip Neri to a Savanorola who, despite his sanctity, began with an external reform: "He burned lites and guitars, looking-glasses and masques, books and pictures in the public square; but Philip bore with every outside extravagance in those whom he addressed, as far as it was not directly sinful, knowing well that if the heart was once set right, the appropriate demeanor would follow."

Savanorola he associated with the pulpit, Philip with the confessional. "Philip had no vocation and little affection for the pulpit. He allured others to the service of God so dexterously, that those who saw it cried out, astonished: Father Philip draws souls as the magnet draws iron."

Newman saw the Church in all her deficiencies, with the eyes of faith. "The heart of every Christian ought to represent in miniature the Catholic Church, since one Spirit makes both the whole Church and every member of it to be in his temple."

Newman insisted that "the Christian Church is simply and literally a party or society instituted by Christ. He bade us to keep together. Fellowship with each other, mutual sympathy, and what spectators from without call party-spirit, all this is a prescribed duty."

Because Newman had so many lay friends, he was especially attentive to their role in the Church. The true signs of God's presence are not necessarily the most useful persons, nor the more favored by God, who make the most noise, or are principals of great changes. "We must be on the lookout for the graces of personal holiness manifested in his elect, which weak as they may seem to mankind, are mighty through God, and have an influence upon the course of his providence."

John Henry Newman's thoughts on spirituality have been gleaned from a book by Father Charles Dessain, titled *The Spirituality of John Henry Newman*. Father Dessain was formerly provost of the Birmingham Oratory, until his death. He edited many of Newman's works, and initiated the process for his canonization in 1958.

In his foreword to Dessain's book, Dr. Nicholas Lash sums up Newman's spiritual life: "Perhaps 'wholeness' is the clue: a preoccupation with personal and intellectual consistency, with the pursuit of a vision of the wholeness of things. This was never an interest in theoretical systems. His deep suspicion of theoretical solutions to practical problems, his horror of inappropriate 'abstraction,' has often provoked the charge that he was 'anti-intellectual.' This is far from the truth.

"Far more than most Catholics of his day, he sought to give informed intellectual enquiry full reign. There were no questions that frightened him. And yet he knew that enquiry only proceeds appropriately when 'earthed' in particular circumstances of practice and experience, inheritance and suffering.

"The 'wholeness' that he sought was a harmony of practice and theory, obedience and enquiry, structure and freedom, sanctity and humanism. And because that 'wholeness' has become, once again, a vision sought by a Church recovering from the one-sidedness of its recent past, a part which has been clericalist in structure, rational in reflection, fearful of contamination by free enquiry and secular culture—the figure of Newman has acquired prophetic significance."

Was John Henry Newman a saint? The youth who discovered his vocation at age fifteen and never turned back? The preacher who proclaimed a lofty doctrine of perfection? The pastor of souls, spiritual father of a religious community in a poor parish of Birmingham? The writer, the journalist, the controversialist, the literary stylist? The friend who chose for his motto for his coat of arms as a cardinal, *Cor Ad Cor Loquitor*, "Heart Speaks to Heart"?

The Church indeed has decided. On January 22, 1991, Pope John Paul II signed the declaration of the heroicity of the virtues of John Henry Newman. From now on Cardinal Newman is entitled to be called Venerable. This completes the first and most important stage on the road to beatification and canonization. It means that in the eyes of the Church, Newman was indeed extraordinarily holy.

When Newman was raised to the cardinalate at age seventy-nine, the letter informing him of the pontiff's intention read: "The Holy Father, deeply appreciating the genius and learning which distinguished you, your piety, the zeal displayed by you in the exercise of the sacred ministry, your devotion and filial attachment to the Holy Apostolic See, and the signal service you have for long years rendered to religion, has decided on giving you a public and solemn proof of his esteem and good will."

Bishop Ullathorne records his visit with a now aged Cardinal Newman. "We had a long and cheery talk, but as I was rising to leave, an action of his caused a scene I shall never forget, for its sublime lesson to myself. He said in low and humble accents, 'My dear Lord, will you do me a great favor?' 'What is it?' I asked. He glided down on his knees, bent down his venerable head, and said, 'Give me your blessing.' What could I do with him before me in a such a posture? I could not refuse without giving him great embarrassment. So I laid my hand on his head, and said, 'My dear Lord Cardinal, notwithstanding all laws to the contrary, I pray God to bless you, and that his Holy Spirit may be full in your heart.'

"As I walked to the door, refusing to put on his biretta, as he went with me, he said, 'I have been indoors all my life, whilst you have battled for the Church in the world.' I felt annihilated in his presence; there is a saint in that man."[7]

When he once heard through a correspondent that he had been called a saint, Newman said, "I have nothing of a saint about me, as everyone knows, and it is a severe (and salutary) mortification to be thought to be next door to one. I may have a high view of many things but it is the consequence of education and a peculiar cast of intellect—but this is very different from being what I admire."[8]

"I have no tendency to be a saint—it is a sad thing to say. Saints are not literary men; they do not love the classics, they do not write tales. I may be well enough in my way, but it is not the 'high line.' People ought to feel this; most people do. But those who are at a distance have a fee-fo-fum notion about me. It is enough for me to blacken the saints' shoes—if St. Philip uses blacking in heaven."[9]

Yet when Cardinal Newman died in 1890, *The London Times* published these words on the day following Newman's death. "Of one thing we may be sure, that the memory of this pure and noble life, untouched by worldliness . . . will endure whether Rome canonizes him or not, he will be canonized in the thoughts of pious people of many creeds in England. The saint . . . in him will survive."

His meteoric career at Oxford University and in the Oxford Movement as an Anglican preacher and tractarian; his dramatic conversion to Catholicism; his ordination as a Catholic priest in Rome; his return to England to establish Oratories in Birmingham and London; his continual engagement in religious controversy until the end; his vindication by Rome when he was named a cardinal at age seventy-nine—all this was the stuff of which holiness was made.

Apart from Newman's holiness, many are recognizing him as a man of our times. Pope John Paul II observed when he visited England in 1982 that "the philosophical and theological thought and spirituality of Cardinal Newman so deeply rooted in and enriched by sacred scripture and the teachings of the Fathers, still retain their particular originality and value." The Pope said that Newman seemed to have a special ecumenical vocation not only for his own country, but for the whole Church and that he seemed to have anticipated the Second Vatican Council when he insisted that "the Church must be prepared for converts as well as converts prepared for the Church."

Cardinal Basil Hume of Westminster has called Newman a saint for our time. "Priestly piety," he wrote, "and zeal, devotion to Christ's Church and love of doctrine—these are, are they not, the hallmark of a great priest? Fidelity to conscience and grace—these are, are they not, marks of the one who humbly and courageously seeks God? Deep intellectual honesty—the characteristic, is it not, of the genuine scholar, the person who is never blind to the simple fact that all truth is, literally of God?"[10]

Finally, an independent witness to Newman's influence, Principal Shairp, Professor of Poetry at Oxford University, but brought up as a Scottish Presbyterian, who writes of Newman:

"Cardinal Newman's mind dwelt much in the remote past; but the objects he there held converse with were of a different order from those which attracted the gaze of Carlyle. . . . He could deal, as his lectures on the Tracts prove, with heroes and conquerors, with great men and the famous in the world's affairs. But the one object which attracted his eye in all the past was the stone hewn out of the side of the mountain which could crush to pieces all the kingdoms of the earth. The kingdom of Christ coming to us from the very time of the apostles, spreading out into all lands, triumphing over a thousand revolutions, exhibiting an awful unity, glorying in a mysterious vitality, so majestic, so imperturbable, so bold, so saintly, so sublime, so beautiful.

"This is the vision which he had ever in his eyes. . . . this was to him no sentimental dream. . . . It was a reality which molded his own character and destiny, and determined the work he set himself to do on earth. He saw, as he believed, a religion prevalent all around, which was secular and mundane, soft and self-indulgent, taking in that part of the gospel which pleased the flesh, but shrinking from its sterner discipline and higher aspirations.

"He made it the aim of his life to introduce some iron into its blood, to impart into the religions of his day something of the zeal, and devotion, and self-denying sanctity, which were the notes of the early faith. The vision which he beheld in the primitive ages he labored to bring home and make practical in these modern times. . . .

"But the world is so set on the genial, not to say jovial, it so loves the padding of material civilization in which it enwraps itself, that it resents any crossing of the natural man, and will always listen greedily to those teachers—and they are many—who persuades it that the flesh ought to have its own way. A teacher so to its mind the world has not found in Cardinal Newman."[11]

Chapter Five

Heart Speaks to Heart

John Henry Newman was a man of many deep and intimate friendships during his long life. He had none of the usual hang-ups about having "a particular friend," which most seminary rectors in years past had. At least many older priests can still recall the many rules about avoiding special friendships in the seminary, such as never going out for a walk two-by-two, or tying a white handkerchief on the doorknob to let others know a friend is visiting your room.

In one of his sermons, Newman discussed "particular friendships." He said: "We find our Savior had a private friend: and this shows us, first, how entirely he was a man, as much as one of us, in his wants and feelings; and next, that there is nothing contrary to the spirit of the gospel, nothing inconsistent with the fullness of Christian love in having our affection directed in a special way toward certain persons. . . . There have been men before now who have supposed Christian love was so diffusive as not to admit of concentration upon individuals. . . . Now I shall here maintain in opposition to such notions of Christian love, and with our Savior's pattern before me, that the best preparation for loving the world at large, and loving it duly and wisely, is to cultivate an intimate friendship and affection toward those who are immediately about us."[1]

Newman felt very strongly that we could not "love all human beings," "love the human race," "be friends with all humankind," except in a vague, benevolent way. Whereas real human love "must depend on practice, and therefore must begin by exercising itself on our friends around us, otherwise it will have no existence."[2]

It is through love of relatives and friends, submission to their wishes, by "bearing with their infirmities, overcoming their occasional waywardness by kindness, by dwelling on their excellence, and trying to copy them" that we form the roots of charity in our hearts.[3]

He was concerned about sacrificing individuals to the general good in our plans of charity, ignoring our friends in any effort at doing good on a large scale, as ambitious persons were wont to do—climbing over our friends to attain a higher goal; cultivating so-called market friendships. Newman sees the tragedy in the end of such behavior of having nothing to rejoice in, or grieve at, nothing to lose or gain in large plans of benevolence, since such schemes were never engaged in for their own sake but only out of expedience.

Newman believes each of us needs to have demands made upon our daily sympathy and tenderness, needs to have someone to comfort or to consult, someone to "indulge the love of variety and the restless humors which are so congenial to the mind of most."[4] In a word, we need friends to interplay and interact with in order to grow in love.

This indeed was one of the arguments for marriage "which not only calls out the tenderest and gentlest feelings of our nature, but, where persons do their duty, must be in various ways more or less a state of self-denial." The same holds for religious communities. "It is difficult" but "good and joyful for brethren to dwell together in unity."[5]

In his classic sermon, "The Parting of Friends," his last sermon as an Anglican before converting to Catholicism, Newman described some of the intimate friendships in the Old and New Testament. His description of David's friendship with Jonathan is touching. "Very pleasant has thou been to me, thy love for me was wonderful, passing the love of women," he quotes David as saying. On parting, David and Jonathan had made a covenant, "Thou shalt not only," said Jonathan, "while yet I live, show me the kindness of the Lord, that I die not; but also thou shall not cut off thy kindness from my house forever. . . . And Jonathan caused David to swear again, because he loved him, for he loved him as he loved his own soul."[6]

He closes his sermon in this beautiful way.

"And O my brethren, O kind and affectionate hearts, O loving friends, should you know anyone whose lot it has been by writing or by word of mouth, in some degree to help you thus to act, if he has ever told you what you knew about yourselves, or what you did not know; has read to you your wants or feelings, and comforted you by the very reading; and has made you feel that there was a higher life than this daily one, and a brighter world than that you see; or encouraged you, or sobered you, or opened a way to the inquiring, or soothed the perplexed; if what he has said or done has ever made you take interest in him, and feel well inclined toward him; remember such a one in time to come, though you hear him not, and pray for him, that in all things he may know God's will, and at all times he may be ready to fulfill it."[7]

A passage that not only describes Newman's friends, but himself as well.

Despite his many friends inside and outside the Catholic Church, Newman remains essentially a lonely, sensitive, misunderstood man during his lifetime, who often had to leave his loves behind in the pursuit of higher duties. He once wrote: "We must always so love our friends as feeling that one day or another we may perchance be called upon to hate them—that is, forget them in the pursuit of higher duties." For him this too was often a self-fulfilling prophecy.

John Henry Newman died August 11, 1890, nearly ninety years old, and was buried August 19 at Rednal, in the same grave as his beloved friend of thirty-two years, Ambrose St. John. Embroidered on his pall was his motto, *Cor Ad Cor Loquitor*, "Heart Speaks to Heart."

The motto best sums up his views on friendship.

There is a collection of photographs of special friends of John Henry Newman arranged on the wall next to the altar of his private chapel, still preserved today as it was the day he died in 1890, at the Birmingham Oratory. For the most part, the photos are of younger men who followed him into the Catholic Church when he converted from Anglicanism in 1845. They served as a prayerful reminder for Newman whenever he celebrated Mass.

Indeed, the sensitive Newman was a man of intense friendships extending from his days at Oxford University, where he attracted a group of young theology students who attempted to establish a middle way between Catholicism and the Low Church of England, Evangelicalism. The self-styled Tractarian Movement—because the authors wrote tracts to express their views—eventually led Newman and many of his friends into the Catholic Church.

There is no doubt that the ascetic Newman was an attractive figure. Aubrey de Vere, a friend, describes his first encounter with the young Newman at Oxford. "The emotion of seeing him for the first time was one of the greatest of my life. I shall never forget his appearance. I had been waiting some time, and then the door opened, and Newman, in cap and gown, entered very swiftly and quietly, with a kind of balance of figure, like a very great lady sweeping into the room. That was my first impression; the second was that of a high bred young monk of the Middle Ages, whose asceticism cannot quite conceal his distinguished elegance."[8]

One of Newman's most intense friendships was with Richard Hurrell Froude, who died at thirty-three in 1836, of consumption. Froude had been involved with Newman in the Oxford Movement before Newman joined the Catholic Church. He had made the tour of the Mediterranean with Newman in 1832, after Newman had given up his position as tutor at Oriel College.

When Newman received word of Froude's death, he wrote to another friend, John Bowden: "He was so very dear to me, that it is an effort to me to reflect on my own thoughts about him. I can never have a greater loss, looking on for the whole of life—for he was to me, and he was likely to be ever, in the same degree of continual familiarity which I enjoyed with yourself in our undergraduate days . . . yet it has pleased God to take him, in mercy to him, but by a very heavy visitation to all who were intimate with him. Yet everything was so bright and beautiful about him, that to think of him must always be a comfort. The sad feeling I have, is that one cannot retain in one's memory all one wishes to keep there and that, as year passes after year, the image of him will be fainter and fainter."[9]

John Bowden, Isaac Williams and William Copeland were to follow Froude's footsteps into Newman's circle of friends for whom Newman "had the love that passes that of common relation." When Bowden got married, it was Ambrose St. John who took his place in Newman's affections, a place he held for thirty-two years. Ambrose joined the Catholic Church with Newman, went to Rome with him to prepare for the priesthood and be ordained in 1846, and served Newman faithfully as a constant companion. Not as well read or as gifted as Newman, Ambrose was unselfish and devoted to Newman to the end.

When Father Ambrose was dying, Newman later wrote, "he got hold of me and threw his arm over my shoulder and brought me to him so closely . . . he got hold of my hand and clasped it so tightly as really to frighten me. I had to get one of the others to unlock his fingers."[10]

The death of Ambrose was a terrible blow for the aging Newman. He wrote to one friend, "I do not expect ever to get over the loss I have had. It is an open wound which in old men cannot be healed."[11]

In his classic work, *Apologia Pro Vita Sua*, his spiritual autobiography written in 1864 in response to some charges made against him by the popular and anti-Catholic Charles Kingsley, Newman spends considerable time writing about the friends along the way who had a powerful influence upon him, both in his Anglican days and in his Catholic years.

"Never man had kinder or more indulgent friends than I have had. . . . Blessings of friends, which to my door, unasked, unhoped, have come. They have come and they have gone; they came to my great joy, they went to my great grief. He who gave took away."[12]

One after another Newman acknowledges the influence of friends along his spiritual journey. To Thomas Scott, whose unworldliness and independence of mind, whose writing he absorbed as an undergraduate, "I almost owe my soul," he writes.[13] From 1822 to 1825, he saw the most of Dr. Whately and Dr. Hawkins, vicar of St. Mary's. "I can say with a full heart that I love him, and have never ceased to love him,"[14] although as head of Newman's College, Hawkins and Newman often disagreed. He was able to shed his Calvinism and develop a sense of Catholic tradition, under Hawkins.

As to Dr. Whately, "I owe him a great deal. He was a man of generous and warm heart. He was particularly loyal to his friends, and to use a common phrase, 'all his geese were swans.' "[15] Awkward and timid in 1822, Newman found Whately a gentle and encouraging instructor who "opened my mind, and taught me to think and to use my reason." Whately taught him much about the existence of the Church as a corporation, and how necessary it was that Church and state should be independent of each other.

During the first years of his residency at Oriel College, from 1823, Newman had the intimacy of a dear and true friend, Dr. Pusey, "a soul so devoted to the cause of religion, so full of good works, so faithful in his affections." Then came two Fellows, Robert J. Wilberforce and Richard Hurrel Froude, and then Keble, who was brought together with Newman by Froude, who considered bringing the two together the one good thing he had done in his lifetime. Keble gave to Newman that "firmness of assent which we give to religious doctrine, not to the probabilities which introduced it, but to the living power of faith and love which accepted it."[16]

Newman writes that Hurrel Froude, who was a pupil of Keble's, was "formed by him, and in turn reacting upon him. I knew him first in 1826, and was in the closest and most affectionate friendship with him from about 1829, till his death in 1836."[17]

"Nor have I here to speak," Newman continues about Froude, "of the gentleness and tenderness of nature, the playfulness, the free elastic force and graceful versatility of mind, and the patient winning considerateness in discussion, which endeared him to those to whom he opened his heart."

It was Froude who introduced Newman to many Catholic ideas, such as the interpretation of scripture, tradition as the main instrument of religious teaching, the excellence of virginity, of whom the Blessed Virgin was the great pattern. "He delighted in thinking of the saints; and he had a keen appreciation of the idea of sanctity. . . . He embraced the principle of penance and mortification. He had a deep devotion to the Real Presence, in which he had a firm faith. He was powerfully drawn to the Medieval Church, but not to the Primitive."[18]

Of course, many of these friends of Newman joined with him in the Oxford Movement, which began on July 14, 1833, when Keble preached the Assize Sermon in the University pulpit.

What shines through these years of Newman at Oxford University leading up to his conversion in 1845 is the close and intimate friendships formed among these Oxford dons that had a human character as well as spiritual and intellectual. These had to be very heartwarming and intellectually stimulating years for the young Doctor Newman, the Anglican priest, and as he brings out in his final sermon at St. Mary's, on "The Parting of Friends," a difficult separation from many of his Anglican friends, as he made his final journey of faith into the bosom of the Catholic Church.

Rejected by many of his Anglican friends at the time of his conversion, and still suspect among Catholics, Newman had the difficult task of beginning anew the final forty-four years of his life as a Catholic.

In the words of Father Gregory Winterton, Provost of the Birmingham Oratory and driving force behind the beatification cause of Newman, "The fidelity of John Henry led him of course, like all holy people, into countless scrapes, frustrations and sufferings. We need only mention a few, at Oriel, Hawkins and Whately; after the publication of Tract 90, the full weight of university authorities, the Anglican Bishops, and many others fell upon him. After he became a Catholic, he still did not escape these hardships: the Achilli trial, his treatment when he was trying to set up the Catholic University in Ireland, the Oratory School, and the Oratory at Oxford are obvious examples, as is Charles Kingsley's attack on him, which was the cause of his writing his *Apologia*. But all of these he accepted cheerfully as an inevitable part of the attempt to follow Christ to which he had set himself."[19]

Despite his difficulties during his Catholic years with Faber, when he was establishing his Oratories in Birmingham and London; with Archbishop Cullen of Ireland, when he tried to establish the Catholic University of Ireland; with Monsignor George Talbot, confident of Pope Pius IX, over some of his positions on the role of the laity in the Church; with Cardinal Edward Manning of Westminster, who was suspect of his orthodoxy; and even with some passing problems with Bishop Ullathorne of Birmingham, to whom Newman remained loyal till the end, Newman maintained some intense and loyal friendships both inside and outside the Catholic Church. The problem was he outlived most of his friends, as old persons are wont to do.

The support he received from the members of the Birmingham Oratory, in particular Ambrose St. John, had to be a great consolation to him during his troublesome years.

Newman closes his *Apologia* with St. Philip's name and on St. Philip's feastday, as a memorial "of affection and gratitude to St. Philip's sons, my dearest brothers of this house, the priests of the Birmingham Oratory, Ambrose St. John, Henry Austin Mills, Henry Bittleson, Edward Caswall, William Paine Neville, and Henry Ignatius Ryder, who have been so faithful to me; who have been so sensitive of my needs; who have been so indulgent of my failings; who have carried me through so many trials; who have grudged no sacrifice, if I asked for it; who have been so cheerful under discouragement of my causing; who have done so many good works, and let me have the credit of them—with whom I have lived so long, with whom I hope to die."[20]

Newman then pays a special tribute to Ambrose St. John "whom God gave me, when he took everyone else away; who are the link between my old life and my new; who have now for twenty-one years been so devoted to me, so patient, so zealous, so tender; who have let me lean so hard upon you; who have watched me so narrowly; who have never thought of yourself, if I was to question."[21]

What a beautiful thought it was for John Henry Newman to have pictures of his friends along the wall of his private chapel in the Birmingham Oratory, to remind him of his friends in his intentions at Mass.

Although considered a minor poet, two of his most famous poems are "The Pillar of the Cloud" and "The Dream of Gerontius." They span his life. The first ("Lead Kindly Light," as it is popularly known), was written in 1833 when Newman was at sea.

Lead, Kindly Light, amidst the encircling gloom
Lead Thou Me On;
the night is dark, and I am far from home
Lead Thou Me On.
Keep Thou my feet,
I do not ask to see the distant scene:
one step enough for me.

"The Dream of Gerontius," a dramatic poem which portrays the death of an old man and what happens to his soul when he enters eternity, was written in 1865, when Newman was sixty-four years old. It was written at the time he finished the *Apologia*, which had been composed at a feverish pitch, as he experienced the feeling of his own approaching death.

In our time, the Dream has been made well known through being set to music by Sir Edward Elgar. In it, Newman, typically, calls on his friends to pray for him. The dying Gerontius strengthened by the sacraments and the prayers of friends, makes his profession of faith, then passes into the next life in the state of grace.

> Praise to the Holiest in the height,
> And in the depth be praise;
> In all his words most wonderful;
> Most sure in all his ways.

The above lyric has also survived as a well-known hymn, taken from the Dream, Praise to the Holiest.

> My work is done,
> My work is o'er
> And so I come
> Taking it home.
> For the crown is won.
> Alleluia.
> For evermore.

Newman was far from dying at age sixty-four. The *Apologia* had put him back in the national spotlight, and he again was more in demand than ever.

Trinity College, in late 1877, invited him back to Oxford to make him its first honorary Fellow. Newman gladly accepted, but it was an emotional moment for him when in early 1878 he returned to Oxford for the first time since 1845. He visited Pusey and saw the new Keble College. He also visited Littlemore.

Not only had the Pillar of the Cloud been lifted at Oxford University, but also in Rome, when in 1879 Pope Leo XIII named Newman a cardinal of the Church. He went to Rome in April 1879, to receive the honor. He was now seventy-eight years old. The cardinalate was not the end, but another beginning for Newman.

Newman was accepted by all of England, as a cardinal, and was even entertained by the President and Fellows of Trinity College, where he preached at the new church of St. Aloysius on the Holy Trinity, in the morning, and on the Lord as shepherd, in the evening. A long way from the days of Tract 90, when he was condemned by the University and banned.

In 1886 Newman began to fail. Newman said his last Mass on Christmas Day 1889. He was too infirm and blind to carry on. On August 11, 1890 at age eighty-nine he died. He had composed a final epithet for himself, in Latin. It expressed his whole life. *Ex umbris et imaginibus in veritatem*, out of shadows and images into the truth.

Notes

Introduction

1. Quoted in John R. Griffin, *The Oxford Movement: A Revision* (Front Royal: Christendom Publications, 1980), 30.

2. Christopher Hollis, "The Secularized Church" in *Newman and the Modern World* (London: Hollis and Carter, 1967), 11.

3. Ibid., 215-16.

4. Ibid., 213.

5. "Letter on the Restoration of the Hierarchy" in J. Coulson, *Newman: A Portrait Restored* (London: Sheed and Ward, 1965).

6. R. Church, *Occasional Papers*, 2 vols., cited in Christopher Hollis, *Newman and the Modern World.*

Chapter 1

1. John Henry Newman, *Apologia Pro Vita Sua, History of My Religious Opinions* (New York: Modern Library, 1950), 70; henceforth *Apologia.*

2. Ibid., 70.

3. Meriol Trevor, *The Pillar of the Cloud* (London: MacMillan Co., 1962), 142

4. *Apologia,* 36.

5. Letter to Rose (May 23, 1836).

6. Michael Rear, *John Henry Newman, 150 Years of the Oxford Movement* (London: Catholic Truth Society, 1983), 10.

7. Bernard Basset, S. J., *Newman at Littlemore* (Birmingham: Friends of Newman Publications), 12.

8. Ibid.

9. Meriol Trevor, *Newman's Journey* (Huntington: Our Sunday Visitor, 1985), 94.

10. Cited in Michael Rear, *John Henry Newman, 150 Years of the Oxford Movement,* 14.

11. *Apologia,* 20.

12. Ibid., chap. 2.

13. Ibid., 58-59.

14. Ian Ker, "Newman's Conversion to the Catholic Church," a paper presented at the Seventh Annual Newman Conference, held in August 1989 at the University of St. Mary of the Lake in Mundelein, Illinois.

15. Ibid.

16. Ibid.

17. Ian Ker and Thomas Gornall, S. J., eds., *Letters and Discourses of John Henry Newman* (Oxford: Clarendon Press, 1979), 3:181, 239.

18. Ibid., 277.

19. John Henry Newman, *Verses on Various Occasions* (London: Longman, Green & Co., 1910), 153.

20. *Apologia*, 53.

21. Ibid., 293-94.

Chapter 2

1. Rev. Anthony Stark, "John Henry Newman: Priest and Oratorian" in Guild of Our Lady of Ransom, *John Henry Newman: A Study on Holiness* (London: Bearleigh Press, 1991), chap. 7.

2. Ibid.

3. Ibid.

4. Ibid.

5. Cited by Meriol Trevor, *The Pillar of the Cloud,* 429.

6. Ibid.

7. Wilfried Ward, *Life and Times of Cardinal Wiseman*, vol. 2 (London: Longman, Green & Co., 1897), 61.

8. Francis J. Donnelly, S. J., ed., *John Henry Newman, The Second Spring* (London: Longman, Green & Co., 1911). The next few quotes are from here.

9. Donald McCarthy and Thomas O'Loughlin, *Cardinal Newman: The Catholic University, A University Commemorative Volume* (Dublin: The University College, 1990), 17.

10. Meriol Trevor, *Newman: Light in Winter* (Garden City: Doubleday & Co., Inc., 1963), 110.

11. Hollis, citing a private paper of Newman in *Newman and the Modern World,* 126.

Chapter 3

1. John Henry Newman, *The Present Position of Catholics in England* (London: Longman, Green & Co., 1908), 390.

2. Charles S. Dessain, *The Spirituality of John Henry Newman* (Minneapolis: Winston Press, 1977), 26.

3. Jean Guitton, *The Church and the Laity* (Montreal: Palm Publishers, 1965), 159.

4. Ibid.

5. Meriol Trevor, *Newman: Light in Winter,* 201.

6. John Henry Newman, *Parochial and Plain Sermons* (San Francisco: Ignatius Press, 1987), 2:258.

7. John Henry Newman, *The Present Position of Catholics in England,* 390.

8. Jean Guitton, *The Church and the Laity,* 154-55.

Chapter 4

1. Eithne M. O'Sharkey, ed., "Discourse and Arguments on Various Subjects" in *Meditations and Prayers from the Writings of Cardinal Newman* (Dublin: Irish Messenger Publications, 1979), 5.

2. Ibid.

3. Friends of Cardinal Newman Association, *Cardinal John Henry Newman: A Study in Holiness* (Huntington: Our Sunday Visitor, 1982), 36.

4. Ibid., 37.

5. Ibid., 32-33.

6. Charles S. Dessain, *The Spirituality of John Henry Newman,* 33. Next few quotes are from this publication.

7. Guild of Our Lady of Ransom, *John Henry Newman: A Study on Holiness* (London: Bearleigh Press, 1991), enlarged edition, 49.

8. Ibid., 86.

9. Ibid., 23.

10. Basil Hume, *Cardinal John Henry Newman: A Saint for Our Times* (London: Guild of Our Lady of Ransom), 1.

11. Gregory Winterton, *Newman: A Saint for Our Times* (Birmingham: Friends of Newman Publications), 1.

Chapter 5

1. John Henry Newman, *Parochial and Plain Sermons,* 2:257.

2. Ibid., 259.

3. Ibid., 219.

4. Ibid., 261.

5. Ibid., 263.

6. *The Works of Cardinal Newman: Sermons Bearing on Subjects of the Day* (Westminster: Christian Classics, 1968), 395.

7. Ibid., 409.

8. Wilfried Ward, *The Life of John Henry Cardinal Newman* (London: Longman, Green & Co., 1912), 1:66.

9. Meriol Trevor, *The Pillar of the Cloud,* 182.

10. Meriol Trevor, *Newman: Light in Winter,* 526.

11. Ibid., 529.

12. *Apologia*.

13. Ibid., 36.

14. Ibid., 39.

15. Ibid., 41.

16. Ibid., 45.

17. Ibid., 52.

18. Ibid., 53-54.

19. Gregory Winterton, *Newman: A Saint for Our Times,* 2.

20. *Apologia,* 275.

21. Ibid.